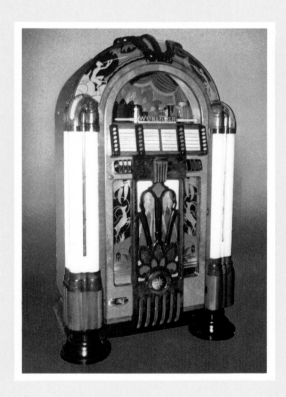

VINTAGE JUKEBOXES

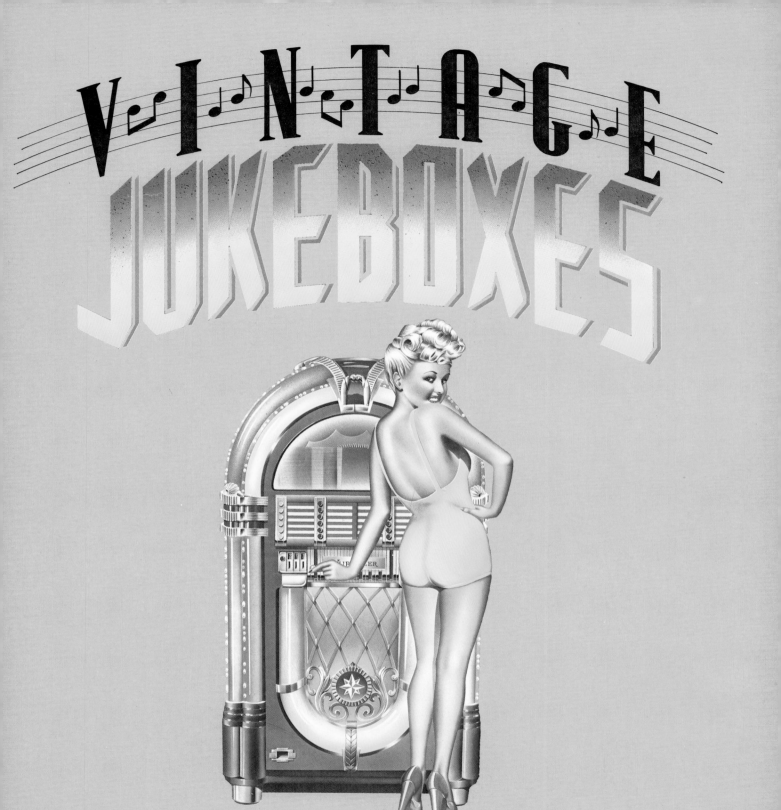

CHARTWELL
BOOKS, INC.

CHRISTOPHER PEARCE

A QUINTET BOOK

Published by Chartwell Books
A Division of Book Sales, Inc.
110 Enterprise Avenue
Secaucus, New Jersey 07094

ISBN 1-55521-323-5

This book was designed and produced by
Quintet Publishing Limited
6 Blundell Street
London N7 9BH

Creative Director: Peter Bridgewater
Art Director: Ian Hunt
Designer: Annie Moss
Editors: Paul Barnett, Patricia Bayer, Judith Simons

Typeset in Great Britain by
Central Southern Typesetters, Eastbourne
Manufactured in Hong Kong by Regent Publishing
Services Limited
Printed in Hong Kong by South Sea Int'l Press Ltd.

CONTENTS

On Main Street—
Highways and Byways

Musical Fun for Everyone

Go where you will. Look and listen as you go. Everywhere people are having fun to Wurlitzer Music.

That's the kind of music it is. Catchy tunes that start you singing. Lively tunes that stimulate fellowship and fun. Popular tunes, the music *of* the people, *by* the top entertainers, *for* your enjoyment.

Next time you go out for food or refreshment, go in where they have Wurlitzer Music. You'll find that good tunes and good times always go together. The Rudolph Wurlitzer Company, North Tonawanda, New York. ★ ★ ★ See Phonograph Section of Classified Telephone Directory for names of Wurlitzer Dealers.

The *Sign of the Musical Note* identifies places where you can have fun playing a Wurlitzer.

THE NAME THAT MEANS *Music* **TO MILLIONS**
The music of Wurlitzer pianos, accordions, commercial phonographs and electronic organs is heard "'round the world." The Rudolph Wurlitzer Company is America's largest manufacturer of pianos all sold under one name...also the nation's largest, best known producer of juke boxes and accordions.

AUTHOR'S PREFACE

Writing the history of the jukebox is a bit like writing a biography. One could start at the moment of conception, then follow the subject's life minute by minute, through birth, the childhood years and so on. Alternatively, one could concentrate on the years of maturity and achievement. In this "biography" of the jukebox I have adopted the latter course.

During the last 20 years or so the "modern" jukebox has lost much of the popularity its predecessors enjoyed, yet this is not to say that the jukebox is dead. Over the years, it has survived many threats – from people who didn't like "jukebox" as a name to those who didn't like jukeboxes at all and wanted not just the name but the device itself abolished. The jukebox has survived times of war and economic depression and the encroachments of other forms of entertainment, such as television; its story must be viewed against a constantly shifting background of social change. So to focus primarily on the "jukebox years," the 1940s and 1950s, is not to dismiss what went before – and certainly not what has come since: too many people in recent years have tried to declare the jukebox dead, but, to paraphrase Mark Twain, reports of its death are an exaggeration. Rather, we are saying that the 1940s and 1950s were the jukebox's finest moments, when designers and engineers worked at breakneck pace to create different models to keep the public amused and stimulated, when every year brought something new – sometimes dramatically so – and when the jukebox was an identifiable part of the "American way of life".

Jukebox history has been shaped largely by the four giants of the industry, AMI, Rock-Ola, Seeburg and Wurlitzer. Rivalry between them generated creative energy and the hothouse atmosphere in which the jukebox grew fast and exotic. Their manufacturing capacity enabled them to spend vast sums on developing a new model and yet, within a year or even less, ditch it in favor of another. With each new model they took a chance, sometimes gaining a market position, sometimes losing out, but all the while trying to gauge the public mood – and, on occasion, shaping it.

In concentrating solely on the work of the Big Four, I have had to ignore many other jukebox companies. My apologies, therefore, to Packard, Filben, Buckley, Aeiron, Evans, Gabels and the Mighty Mills; all are part of the jukebox story, but in the final judgment they cannot be regarded as history makers.

Wherever possible, the illustrations in this book have been taken from the original brochures and advertisements of the period. These often beautiful documents can be even rarer than the machines they portray. Like the jukeboxes themselves, they are survivors of a past age, one which they encapsulate and preserve.

LEFT *The 1948 Wurlitzer Model 1100 was Paul Fuller's final jukebox design and the last to be given a "popular" advertising campaign.*
BELOW *Seeburg's Model 220, introduced in 1959, incorporated stereo sound.*

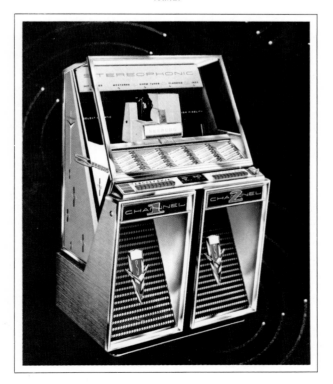

"A stone's throw from the White House" is Brownie's Grill on Pennsylvania Avenue in Washington, D. C. "Rock-Ola Dial-A-Tune remote control and the Rock-Ola Master Model phonograph are playing an important part in stimulating business," says Mr. Brown, owner.

Rock-Ola Dial-A-Tune Remote Control installation in Chicago's famous Sugar Bowl Tavern where the crowds gather from 8 A.M. 'till. . . . This Dial-A-Tune installation consisted of seven wall boxes and two bar boxes.

8

INTRODUCTION

This book is an affectionate tribute to the machine which was, during the 1940s and 1950s, the single most loved – and sometimes hated – symbol of its era. Once a feature of thousands of bars and diners throughout the United States, its familiarity made it a friend, while the magic of individual styling insured that it always retained its mystery. It was the jukebox into which the lonely trucker at the coffee shop dropped his nickel to inspire dreams of his baby back home, the jukebox that the kids made for in Chuck Berry's song when they wanted to hear something really hot, the jukebox that linked communities whose local operator stocked it with songs and dances from the old country. . . .

Rich sounds from these luxurious machines transformed the atmosphere. Thousands of romances (and the occasional fight) started in the jukebox's glow. And in later years, when the colors faded, the cabinets became scruffy, the glasses were broken, the bright metal tarnished and the jukeboxes were finally unplugged to be carted away into storage or trashed, it was as though something had, almost unnoticed, died.

Yet their magic had not died with them. Today they are being rediscovered, rescued from their dusty retirement, lovingly restored and refurbished and brought into homes, and sometimes put to work in bars and restaurants. They are welcomed back, even by those who were not even born when the jukebox enjoyed its heyday.

This book has been written at a time that may one day be looked back upon as a turning point in the history of the jukebox. Technology has brought us the CD jukebox, in its way the ultimate achievement of jukebox development. At the same time two major manufacturers, Rock-Ola and Wurlitzer, have brought out successful modern reproductions of old-style machines – the old machines themselves being art collectibles today. This new status is a recognition of the uniqueness and magnificence of the old jukeboxes, yet at the same time it denies them their real glory – the fact that, for roughly a quarter of a century, commercially designed and mass-produced objects, some beautiful, some ugly, some zany, sometimes masterpieces of engineering and sometimes not, found a place in people's hearts and minds and imaginations.

There is currently no jukebox museum, so let this book serve as a sort of "Jukebox Hall of Fame." As you turn the silent pages, you may start imagining that you are hearing the sounds of Glenn Miller, Bing Crosby, the Andrews Sisters, Chuck Berry, Muddy Waters, Hank Williams, Elvis Presley, Buddy Holly. . . .

The jukebox is not dead, long live the jukebox!

BELOW *The manual-selection version of AMI's J200, introduced in 1959. In terms of hard, uncompromising styling, AMI at this time was probably closer to the spirit of the imminent 1960s than any other jukebox manufacturer.*

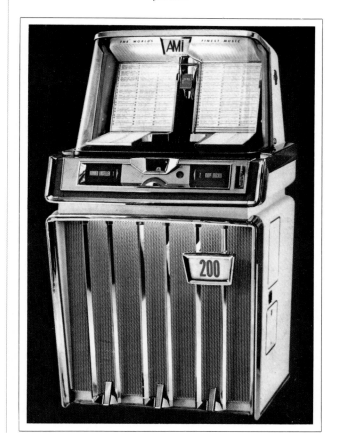

1 A STAR IS BORN

t is tempting to see the history of technology in comic-strip terms. A Fred Flintstone character chips away at a boulder and the wheel is invented, Archimedes leaps out of his bath, an apple lands on Isaac Newton's head, Sam Colt watches a ship's wheel spin – it all seems so simple. Unfortunately, no one ever walked into a patent office and said they had just invented the jukebox. As with so many other and more major historical events, an interlocking pattern of events and developments was responsible for the emergence of the jukebox.

Coin-operated music had been around since the 19th century in the form of musical boxes, player pianos and, at the end of the century, the Edison cylinder phonograph. But the fact that it is coin-operated is only one aspect of the jukebox. What are the others? Well, a jukebox should by definition have a selection of music, that music being in the form of a phonograph record. This stage of development was attained in 1906, when a coin-operated record player with an automatic changer system – the "Gabel Automatic Entertainer" – was brought out by the John Gabel Company. An acoustic, mechanical device, like the home record players of its day, it had to be wound up: the sound came out of a horn speaker. Further progress toward the jukebox proper was not possible until the 1920s, with the advent of electrically recorded and played records. By the end of this decade, jukeboxes were being manufactured by Gabel, Mills Novelty Company, Holcombe & Hoke, the Automatic Musical Instrument Company (AMI) and Seeburg.

An employee of Holcombe & Hoke, Homer Capehart – later to be instrumental in Wurlitzer entering the jukebox business – branched out on his own as the Capehart Automatic Phonograph Company. Thus, three important companies in jukebox history – AMI, Seeburg and Capehart – date back to the earliest days. Wurlitzer started manufacturing jukeboxes in 1933; and Rock-Ola followed in 1935. Out of the Big

Four primarily responsible for the development and then survival of the jukebox, only Rock-Ola was a newcomer to the mechanical music industry: the company's background was in scale and games manufacture. By contrast, AMI had emerged from the National Piano Manufacturing Co. (producers of player pianos), Seeburg was a manufacturer and distributor of player pianos and orchestrions, and Wurlitzer had established a reputation as a maker of pianos, organs and radios.

BELOW *Now best remembered as the starting point in the business for Homer Capehart, Holcombe & Hoke were successful pioneer manufacturers of jukeboxes.*

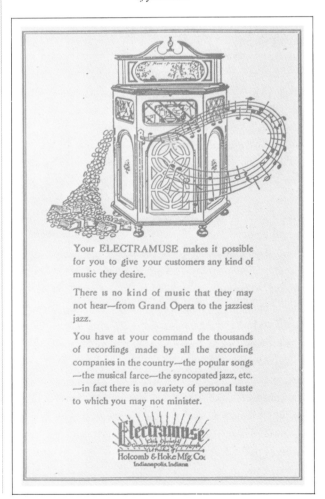

Your ELECTRAMUSE makes it possible for you to give your customers any kind of music they desire.

There is no kind of music that they may not hear—from Grand Opera to the jazziest jazz.

You have at your command the thousands of recordings made by all the recording companies in the country—the popular songs —the musical farce—the syncopated jazz, etc. —in fact there is no variety of personal taste to which you may not minister.

Electramuse
Coin Operated
Holcomb & Hoke Mfg. Co.
Indianapolis, Indiana

ABOVE *An ancestor of the jukebox, a 19th-century German-made musical box. The walnut cabinet, containing the autochange mechanism, with twin combs and a selection of 10 discs, is mounted on a matching stand.*

The heart of the jukebox is its changer system, whereby records are stored, picked out to be played on the turntable, and then returned. Wurlitzer used the "Simplex" system, in which the records were kept in a stack of trays. The selected tray would swing out over the turntable, which would rise up to take the disc and carry it to the pickup arm, which would swing over to play it. The mechanism could be seen through a window, and the synchronization of these movements was fascinating to watch. Wurlitzer maintained throughout the 1940s and 1950s that the visible record changer was an essential feature of the jukebox. They may have been right for, to many people, the jukebox essentially "died" when the record could no longer be seen playing. Although the changer was on view all through the 1950s, this was

by no means always the case in the 1940s. Rock-Ola, whose Multi-selector system was similar to Wurlitzer's, enclosed the mechanism until 1946 (with the exception of the countertop models of 1939 and 1940). Seeburg, junking its first mechanism (the Wilcox, in which the tone arm moved between a stack of spaced records) in favor of the "Freborg" system, where the records were slid out of a rack onto the turntable, had the mechanism on show between 1935 and 1938, but it then remained hidden until 1948, when a new and very visual changer replaced it. AMI had by 1927 a record changer so basically sound that it lasted them, with minor modification, through to 1957! In this modified system (the principle of which was later to

BELOW *The "Wilcox" stacked-record system replaced Seeburg's earlier Ferris-wheel mechanism. Used only during 1934–5 it was discarded in favor of the reliable "Freborg" sliding trays.*

The Mills' advertisements heralded the repeal of Prohibition: "Large production caused by the return of beer and drink, new inventions and improvements by our alert engineers now make it possible to sell this magnificent instrument at about one-third what ordinary phonographs cost four years ago."

be adopted by Seeburg), the records were stored in a static rack along which the entire record player moved, the record being picked out of the rack by a mechanical arm (the gripper bow) which placed it on the turntable. Although the final qualities which were to be the essence of the "real" jukebox – light, color and extreme styling – were yet to come, by 1935 all four of the major companies were in production with the changer system that would see them through the Golden Age of the 1940s and (with the exception of Seeburg) into the 1950s.

Somewhere along the line the machine had acquired its name. No one can say where or when the word "jukebox" arrived. Generally accepted theories are that it was corrupted from the word "jook," an old black slang term for dancing; the source of the music – gramophone or automatic instrument – would therefore quite naturally have been called the "jook-box." An alternative theory is that "jook" meant "sex," and

that the "jook-box" was the music system used in bordellos. Or again, more innocently, others trace the term back to "jute": "jute joints" were where the jute-picking laborers relaxed and danced.

The music of Wurlitzer pianos, accordions, and juke boxes is heard "'round the world." Wurlitzer is America's largest manufacturer of pianos all produced under one name ... also America's largest manufacturer of accordions and juke boxes.

ABOVE *In this 1945 advertisement, the jukebox shared equal status with Wurlitzer's pianos and accordions.*

Whatever the case, "jazz" slang became a popular affectation during the 1920s and, with Prohibition making many otherwise respectable citizens into criminals (at least technically), the public was increasingly exposed to the influences of the "low-life." Early jukeboxes had been a feature of speakeasies. Following repeal, the manufacturers looked to a vastly expanded market. The post-Prohibition advertisements were specific as to the increased demand for jukeboxes that repeal would bring:

ABOVE *The 1937 Wurlitzer Model 316 was styled in much the same way as the radio consoles of the time.*

Music calls for drinking and dining and dancing calls for more drinking. Trade increases from one hundred to four hundred per cent after the Dance Master is installed. [Mills]

Operate in Music because: Music is not a fad; Repeal has brought a permanent demand on a big scale for coin-operated music . . . [Wurlitzer]

Although the role the jukebox had played in the speakeasy days was tacitly acknowledged by the manufacturers, it was an image they wanted to leave behind them: the word "jukebox" had gathered disreputable associations. Nevertheless, the name stuck: by the 1940s Wurlitzer was describing itself as "the nation's largest, best known producer of jukeboxes."

Jukeboxes of the mid-1930s were housed in heavy walnut cabinets, sometimes enlivened with patterned inlays of veneer. Seeburg produced several cabinets with pronounced Art Deco styling: noteworthy is the 1937 Model Q, which anticipated Wurlitzer in its arched-top design. However, the overall impression of the period is of rather big radio consoles.

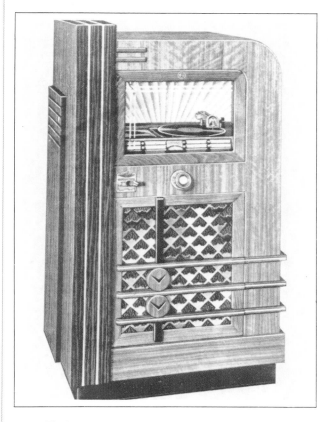

ABOVE *The Seeburg Model J (1937) featured an unusual asymmetrical cabinet showing obvious influences of Art Deco architecture.*

All this was to change with the advent of the "light-up" cabinet. At this time the style known as Modernism was coming into vogue, and plastic was beginning to replace glass as a material for domestic and architectural light fittings. Two of the Big Four jukebox manufacturers were employing innovative young industrial designers to style their cabinets – Nils

ABOVE: *Paul Fuller's first light-up, the Model 24, heralded Wurlitzer's "romantic" era. Ribbed, pale-green plastic was used for the corner pilasters, which were back-lit to produce a warm yellow glow.*

Miller at Seeburg and Paul Fuller at Wurlitzer. Both seized upon the new styling opportunities that light-up plastic presented.

Wurlitzer's Model 24 (1937) featured corner pilasters of ribbed pale green plastic which, when back-illuminated, glowed a warm yellow. The speaker grille was likewise a radical departure from the normal wooden version: set against a deep red speaker cloth was a stylized Art Deco motif of curved Lucite (semi-transparent plastic) rods framed by concertinaed panels of gold "Lectrosheet" (a sort of metal-flake finish). The cabinet stood on "moderne" caster mounts that were incorporated into the bottom part of the machine. Wurlitzer was justifiably proud of this totally original concept of jukebox styling — and of Paul Fuller who was, unusually, given public credit for it in the advertisements:

. . . styled by Paul M. Fuller, one of America's foremost designers, the new Wurlitzer Models 24 and 24A are the most magnificent examples of light and color applied to cabinet decoration ever introduced in the music industry. Added eye appeal means greater play appeal. Play appeal spells greater profits!

ABOVE: *The 1938 "Crown," one of the first of the illuminated Seeburgs. With its sturdy elegance and dearth of ornamentation, it relied on high-quality sound reproduction and engineering rather than on ostentatious display.*

Unlikely though it was that at that stage anyone could have foreseen the heights of decorative jukebox art Fuller was to bring to Wurlitzer, the Model 24 opened up a new dimension. It represented the start of what was to become the Golden Age of the jukebox; from then on the key to the art would be a combination of color, light and form, a combination that transformed the jukebox from a mechanical music

ABOVE *For a total of $114.95 this 1940 Gerber & Glass conversion kit transformed the 1937 Wurlitzer 616 into a light-up, with "Marblette" plastics and the "Heads-up" illuminated selector produced by Homer Capehart's Packard Manufacturing Company.*
TOP *The 1938 Rock-Ola "Monarch" featured the "Borealis" light-up grille as well as an illuminated record changer.*

machine into a visual entertainment. Another reason why this model made history was that it offered 24 selections rather than the 12 or 16 supplied by previous models – "the broadest selection ever offered in any automatic phonograph" read the advertisements. It seemed a lot of music in those days, and Homer Capehart saw it as the ultimate: "That's all the music we'll ever need on a jukebox," he remarked. Within four years Seeburg was to embark on a research project which would ultimately prove him wrong, but throughout the Golden Age Wurlitzer's 24 were to be the greatest number of selections on offer. Rock-Ola claimed that market research had confirmed that 20 selections was the ideal number; AMI, Seeburg and Mills likewise offered 20 selections.

In the wake of Wurlitzer's 1937 Model 24, everyone was demanding light-ups. Seeburg brought out the "Regal", "Crown" and "Concert Grand" models in 1938, adopting a different styling concept from Fuller's. Rather than emphasize the brightening effect of illumination, Seeburg integrated illuminated panels to stress the structural qualities of the cabinet. The favorite color was ruby red: the combination of the use of this color with the concealment of the record changer gives these jukeboxes a mysterious glowing presence. For 1938 Rock-Ola left the changer on view, and accented it with increased lighting, at the same time illuminating the speaker grille with colored light reflected off chrome-plated grille rods – an idea later to be used by Seeburg in its 1952 100C.

AMI, too, brought out a light-up, the "Streamliner", in which the wooden cabinet was reduced to the minimum and the sides, top area and grille were all illuminated. A particularly innovative feature of this machine was that the title cards were incorporated into the selector buttons, which were also back-lit. The grille consisted of two "Deco-style" panels flanking a central column of illuminated plastic, a design later to be seen in both Wurlitzer and Rock-Ola machines. Such was the demand for this new look that a spate of conversion kits appeared on the

ABOVE *With the advent of modernizing kits, the design qualities of the original jukebox were totally lost. Even Wurlitzer's Model 24, which three years previously had revolutionized cabinet design, was to fall victim to modernization (**MIDDLE**). Surely one of the most drastic conversion kits of all, this $39.50 outfit (**LEFT**) claimed to be able to transform all 12- and 16-play console Wurlitzers into countertops!*

market. Seeburg brought out a "universal cabinet," in which an older machine could be re-housed; other conversions involved hacking bits out of cabinets and inserting light-up panels, while yet others were con-cerned with "add on" light features.

From here on, jukebox design became increasing-ly varied and colorful. "Modernizing" kits offered a way in which operators could upgrade their machines without buying new ones. A major difference was that during the late 1930s and the 1940s these kits were all about adding more light and ornamentation, but during the 1950s the situation was reversed: modernization was all about trimming off and sim-plifying. This attitude led to the destruction of many

future classics; but at the time, however, the new jukebox designs were merely the means to a livelihood.

The glamour of illuminated plastic freed the juke-box from the restraints of the old wooden-cabinet format. Yet one of the most amazing designs of the period — the AMI "Singing Towers" (1939) — used glass rather than plastic. Apart from its record changer — which, as with the "Streamliner," could turn the record as it came out of the rack so that it was placed on the turntable to play the "A" or "B" side of the disc — "Singing Towers" might have been made any time during the previous 10 years. Based on "skyscraper" architecture, the panels and dome of "Singing Towers" are of thick molded glass. Despite

ABOVE *Its "skyscraper" lines echoed in the rare extension speaker, AMI's "Singing Towers" can be seen as the forerunner of Rock-Ola's "Spectravox."*

its height, the mechanism takes up only a small part of the interior; nevertheless, the jukebox had to be tall as the speaker was mounted in the top of the main section, behind the button bank and facing upward. The sound was projected into the glass dome on the top and then bounced back through the "Singing Towers" screens. Available also with a "Tower" remote speaker, this sound system was later to be used by Rock-Ola. AMI declined to follow up the Towers concept, and during the next couple of years concentrated instead on a "piped" music system.

Another company that briefly made its mark during the early light-up days was Mills. One of the oldest companies in automatic music, Mills was best known for its violin and player-piano combination, the "Virtuoso," which from 1911 until the advent of

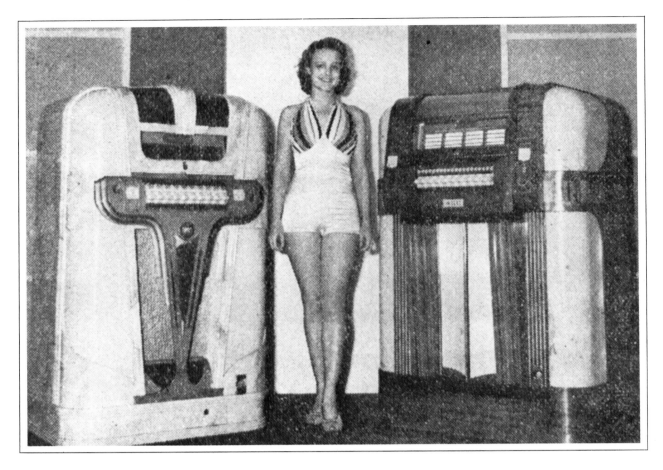

ABOVE *The machine on the left is the "Empress," that on the right the "Throne of Music." Between them is "Mills' Queen of Sweet Music," Sally Somers. She "sanctions these two Mills machines for today's dansportation. 'I get acquainted with the bands and orchestra leaders thru the records,' says Sally."*

electrical reproduction in the 1920s enjoyed considerable popularity. The Mills company was also a major manufacturer of slot machines. As with Wurlitzer and Seeburg, Mills realized that the more sophisticated reproduction offered by electrically recorded music would soon make player pianos obsolete, and so in 1926 they went into jukeboxes; through the late 1920s and early 1930s the company produced a range of successful machines. Mills was never as committed to the jukebox as Wurlitzer, Rock-Ola, AMI and Seeburg, but in 1939 the company brought out two models – the "Empress" and the "Throne of Music" – which, at least in terms of styling, stand equal to their contemporaries. Streamlined in the same manner as the locomotive fronts of the time, the "Empress" featured massive light-up plastics that took up almost the entire front of the cabinet. This model is particularly noted for its

beautifully styled metal grille: finished in dark bronze, sculpted in the "Aztec" Deco style, it rose up from almost a point at its base to become a series of narrow chevrons pierced with illuminated panels. Near the top the lines became flowing, and curved out to incorporate the instruction windows, record-playing indicator and, on either side of the button bank, the coin entry. The "Throne" had a simpler shape, but featured a cabinet enlivened with marquetry bands of veneer. Its chief styling feature was a concave V-shaped speaker screen – a design feature that Wurlitzer would adapt in the 1950s. However, the promise of these two Mills jukeboxes was not to be fulfilled: although a further model went into production, Mills went out of business in 1948.

RIGHT *The 1940 Rock-Ola "Super Luxury Light-up" had, in addition to its main 15-inch speaker, a top-mounted eight-inch speaker hinged so that it could lie flat on the cabinet if not required.*

ABOVE *The telephone-dial selector system of the Rock-Ola "dial-a-tune" wall box was a novelty which insured its success.* BELOW *The 1940 Rock-Ola "Junior" counter model. When mounted on its speaker stand, as here, it became in effect a self-contained miniature jukebox.* RIGHT *This "Junior", placed on the counter, has its speaker on the back wall. Rock-Ola recommended: "Place the speaker up high so the place of business can have volume without having it blare right at the patrons."*

Rock-Ola and Wurlitzer, like Seeburg, had arrived at a point which would determine their design image for the pre-war Golden Age. Rock-Ola's "Luxury Light Up" (1939) served as the basis for successive models throughout the period. As in the Seeburg machines, the mechanism was enclosed, and heavy round-shouldered plastics were incorporated into the design so that they appeared to be set in the casework. For 1939 Rock-Ola brought out a countertop model as well: designated the CM-39, it reappeared with minor styling changes as the 1940 "Junior." Neither model had an integral loudspeaker, instead playing through a speaker that was either wall-mounted or incorporated in the stands made to complement the countertop. Following Seeburg's lead, Rock-Ola brought out a wallbox to be used in conjunction with console models; although this had the novelty of having a telephone-dial selection control, rather than a customary push-button one, it was not as sophisticated as Seeburg's wireless system. Nevertheless, it was very successful.

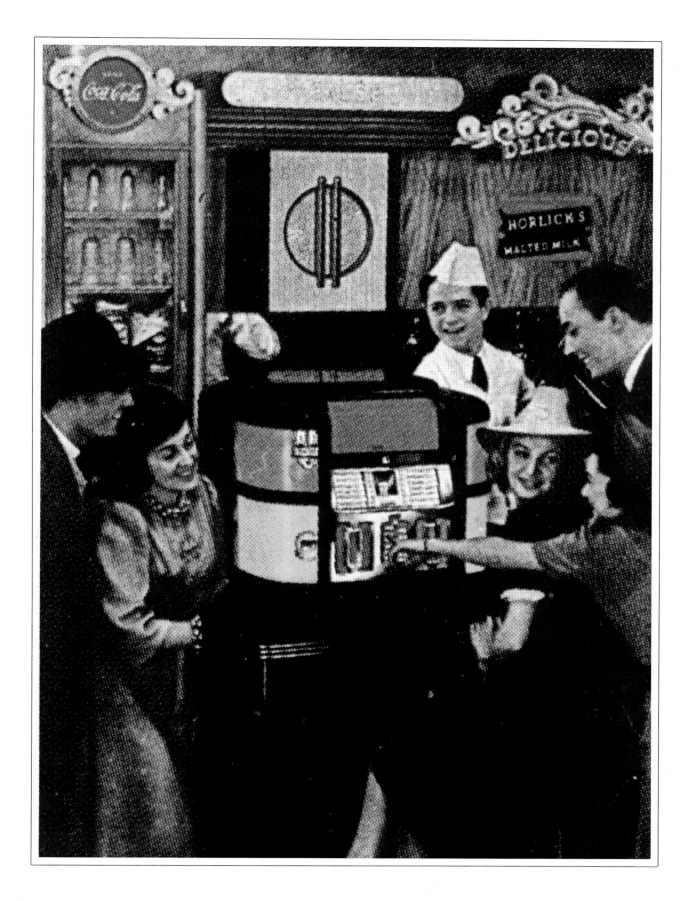

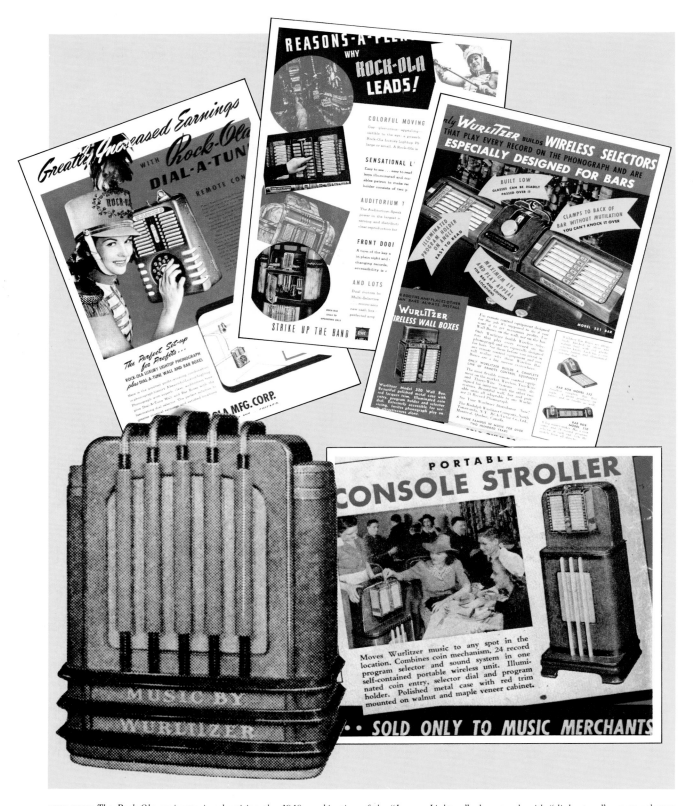

TOP LEFT *The Rock-Ola majorette is advertising the 1940 combination of the "Luxury Light-up" phonograph with "dial-a-tune" remote selectors.* **TOP MIDDLE** *"Strike up the band – it's Rock-Ola for '40."* **TOP RIGHT** *The 1940 Wurlitzer range of remote selectors included the Model 332, "the smallest Bar Box made."* **ABOVE LEFT** *The 1940 Model 350 speaker utilized the site current and was thus "wireless," as opposed to the externally identical Model 250, which was wired direct to the jukebox.* **ABOVE RIGHT** *Like Seeburg, Wurlitzer used the idea of the wandering wall box or "stroller," which could be wheeled up to the patron.*

ABOVE *A decorative metal grille and cabinet castings show the Wurlitzer Model 600 as the transitional stage between the Model 24 and the extravagant designs of the 1940s.*

By now, despite having come into the business late and lacking the "musical" background of the other companies, Rock-Ola was the dominant force in jukeboxes, outselling all others. To Wurlitzer this situation was probably more unacceptable than the traditional competition from old-time rivals such as Seeburg. Having unsuccessfully sued Rock-Ola over alleged patent infringements, Wurlitzer embarked upon a series of styles and models against which no one else could hope to compete. Between 1938 and 1942 they produced no less than 13 different styles of jukebox – not counting model variations! Credit for

this goes to three people: Farny Wurlitzer himself, who, as the black sheep of the family, was determined that his jukebox division should prove as important as Wurlitzer's "respectable" piano, organ and musical-instrument productions; Homer Capehart, who, although he had left Wurlitzer in 1938, had given the company an efficient, loyal distribution set-up and a sense of corporate identity; and Paul Fuller, who brought to the jukebox poetry and romance and whose work, for many, is considered to be the pure essence of 1940s style.

After the success of the 1937 Model 24, Wurlitzer took a year off: its "1938" models were in fact introduced in mid-1939. This pause enabled them to prepare for 1940, which saw four new models. The 1938–9 series, the 500, 600 and Model 61 countertop, therefore represent no more than the tip of the iceberg. Although Wurlitzer had already produced the first countertop jukebox in 1937 (Model 51), this had drawn its styling from a period which the console model of that same year had made obsolete – i.e., – a plain wooden cabinet. The Model 61 was, by contrast, a light-up. It became very popular, and paved the way for the three countertops produced in the 1940s.

Of Wurlitzer's 1939 console models, the Model 600 showed its derivation from the Model 24 but, in its distinctive styling of the front grille, opened up another aspect of what was to become the "Wurlitzer look." Here the Lucite rods had been reduced to straight green verticals, but they were flanked by an elaborate grille of nickel-plated Art Deco-type scrolls. The metallic panels of the Model 24 were replaced by curved panels of marbled plastic, giving the entire grille area not only luminescence but, more importantly, elaborate decoration. The slightly larger deluxe version, the Model 500, featured in its side plastics an additional innovation that was to become an essential Wurlitzer element: movement. Behind the plastics, colored cylinders slowly revolved, animating the jukebox with patterns of light and color.

2 THE WURLITZER YEARS

f the 1940s can be described as the Golden Age of the jukebox, the years 1940 to 1942 must surely represent the mother lode. These were the "Wurlitzer Years," when Paul Fuller, having established the groundwork with the models 24, 500 and 600, freed himself from the constraints of the traditionally proportioned Wurlitzer cabinets. Fuller's work was not essentially sculptural; designs such as the AMI "Singing Towers," the Rock-Ola "Commando" or the Seeburg "Trash Can" would have been beyond his aesthetic scope. However, he was *the* master of the theatrical, romantic look, using wood, metal, plastic, color, lighting and animation in a way that made the entire jukebox the entertainment, not just the music it played.

ABOVE *Anticipating the Model 850, Wurlitzer used the "Peacock" image in their 1940 advertisements. It was an appropriate symbol for the company's "romantic" age.*

ABOVE *The Models 700 and 800, produced by Wurlitzer in 1940.*

Viewed straight-on, there was little to distinguish the 1940 Model 700 from the 1939 Model 600. The coin slides were now in the center of the machine, above the grille, which was a series of curls and circles, very much in the Art Deco tradition of the United States referred to in the designs of the previous two models. The grille rods were moved to either side of the metal-work, thereby directing attention to it. In many jukeboxes, but most particularly Wurlitzers, the grille is the most important single area of the design. Although in Wurlitzers much was made of

the visible record changer, it is to the grille, shielding the source of the music itself, that the eye is drawn.

The Model 700's side pilasters, grandly described in the brochures as "rich Italian onyx" but in reality made of a delicately marbled plastic, were light in color, so that the jukebox could be customized through the installation of colored bulbs. In fact, the sides constituted the most original feature of this model. Up to then (with the exception of "Singing Towers") jukeboxes had been, in terms of decorative elements, rather two-dimensional: they were cabinets with fancy façades. Now Fuller was developing the sides of the cabinet. Toward the top he extended the pilasters back, and he added further panels almost right across the sides.

To complement the Model 700 was the even grander Model 800, which can in many ways be regarded as a scaled-up version. Physically the biggest Wurlitzer up to then, its size, weight and general proportions combined to give it superb sound reproduction. The 800 differs from the 700 also in the details of the front grille, which is reminiscent of that of the earlier Model 500, but with an important innovation. Between the two metal sections of the grille was a vertical panel of fluted plastic, behind which

ABOVE *"Glamor lighting," visible record changer and 24 selections – a combination unique to Wurlitzer.*

In 1941, Wurlitzer completely abandoned the conventionally shaped cabinet. Nothing was to be allowed to stand in the way of making the jukebox as visually entertaining as possible. The Model 750 was the first of the arched-top Wurlitzers. About two-thirds of the façade of the machine was taken up by the front door, an oval shape that matched the curve of the top of the cabinet. The coin slides occupied the space in the middle of this oval, rising out of a fan of light and flanked by the short bubble tubes. Beneath the door, a simple but effective grille displayed the outlines of

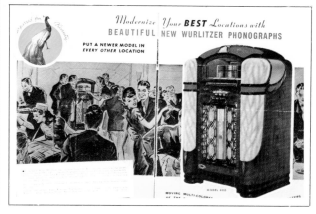

ABOVE AND BELOW *The first jukebox to use "bubble tubes" – described in the advertisements as "liquid fire" – the Model 800 was one of the most imposing Wurlitzers ever.*

were three illuminated "bubble tubes." These were to become a regular feature of the 1940s Wurlitzers, but one can imagine how dramatic the effect was when they first appeared. The technology involved was simple, and had been in common use before, generally in novelty items such as Christmas decorations. A tube of glass (similar to the tube of a neon light) was filled with a liquid whose boiling point was extremely low. At one end of the tube, trapped by an indentation, were bumpers (little granules). The liquid, warmed by a small heating device, boiled, so that bubbles of gas released from the bumpers traveled up the tube. As the tube was completely sealed there was no evaporation: the gas was constantly recycled in a succession of sparkling champagne-type bubbles. You can still sometimes find Wurlitzers whose original bubble tubes are in full working order, despite the fact that they are fast approaching their 50th birthday!

As well as the "dancing bubbles," the Model 800 made a feature of the outer pilasters, breaking up the colored light with zebra-patterned screens to produce a sort of wavy, flickering effect. As a harbinger of the future, the brochures for both the 700 and the 800 featured a picture of a peacock.

Wurlitzer advertisements emphasized the "luxury" qualities of the Model 800. The patrons were designed to match!

flower petals set against a grid: the "petals" were backed with grille cloth and the grid was an open basket-weave of plastic, through which light glowed from behind. An unusual feature of this model was that the grille was made of wood. The plastics were in a pale greenish cream, but they were back-painted in patches of color – usually red, green and yellow – to produce a multicolored glow. Halfway through the year, a further variation was introduced: electric selection. The first model featuring this was called the 750E.

For additional gaiety the Model 750 had an optional animated back mural. This was a fretwork screen with plastic panels, illuminated by a small rotating color cylinder. The standard version had a printed mural of peacock feathers.

But the innovations of the Model 750 were small fry in comparison to those of the two other console models Wurlitzer brought out that year. The most radical departure from any preconception of what a jukebox should be was the Model 780, available with either mechanical or electric selection. More than any other manufacturer, Wurlitzer had always projected the image of the "high-class" jukebox, trying to persuade operators that a Wurlitzer could be located in establishments which would have considered a run-of-the-mill jukebox as the ultimate anathema. Up to now Wurlitzer had based its marketing strategy on emphasizing the luxury of its machines – the quality of the cabinet finish, the "glamour lighting," and so on. Always, however, the design influences had been biased toward Art Deco or Moderne, and juke-

ABOVE *Despite the admen's pictures of opulence, the jukebox was more often a low-budget entertainment. This 1940 photograph was taken in Joe & Louie's Niteclub, described as one of the hotspots for the younger crowd in Houston, Texas. Wurlitzer's district manager of the day, who used this picture for publicity, commented: "These kids can't afford high-priced entertainment, but they can afford to enjoy Wurlitzer music and you can bet it affords them plenty of pleasure. All the best name bands in America play for their dancing and these young folks keep this Model 800 in action practically all the time. It is typical of many Wurlitzers in this territory catering to the younger crowd with sensational success."*

boxes in these styles were simply not acceptable in the more conservative locations. In the early 1940s in the United States there was a burgeoning interest in early American styles: this was partly a reaction against European antiques – which, usually in the form of the most ostentatious of 18th-century French furniture, had been imported in vast quantities by turn-of-the-century millionaires – and partly against the Moderne school, which was likewise of European origin. Magazine articles featured homes whose decor was based on a Colonial theme, and this style was adopted also by bars and restaurants seeking an up-market image.

In an attempt to make inroads into the more conservative establishments, Wurlitzer brought out the first self-effacing jukebox – a sort of "non-jukebox." With great attention to detail, Paul Fuller designed the Model 780 so that it resembled a "Governor Winthrop" cupboard. Only the visible mechanism, title strips, selector keys and coin slides revealed

ABOVE RIGHT *Hip cat! No chance snap this: photographer Harold F. Tenney had noticed that the flipped feline took up the same nonchalant pose in front of the jukebox night after night.*

RIGHT *Its compact size and colorful appearance made the Model 750 one of the most popular pre-war Wurlitzers.*

pewter, was kept to a minimum, and the lock surrounds and hinges were given 18th-century American styling. In keeping with the "period" details, the sides of the jukebox simulated planks "joined" by butterfly pegs. The casework was mahogany-colored and finished with less gloss than normal, in keeping with the antique look. As a cabinet it was magnificent: it would not have looked out of place in the furniture section of a high-class department store (Paul Fuller, before joining Wurlitzer, had after all been head of the interior-design department at Marshall Field, in Chicago). As a jukebox, however, it was an abject failure. People who wanted a jukebox expected it to look like one. People who did not want a jukebox refused to be seduced by an object masquerading as something else.

Despite fancy promotion, showing the *beau monde* in evening dress admiring a Wurlitzer, to many people the image of the jukebox was still tarnished through its association with the old speakeasy days. The jukebox industry as a whole generally suffered bad press (the influential *Chicago Tribune* was a particularly strident critic), and this not only hampered the manufacturers' attempts to gain new sites for their machines but also had a general demoralizing effect.

ABOVE *The Wurlitzer Model 780. As an interior decorator's piece of pastiche it was brilliant. As a jukebox it failed.*

that this was not a cabinet but a jukebox. The front grille, entirely of wood, took the form of a wheel, with finely turned spokes and a carved center. Behind it, the speaker screen was made of cotton, printed in squares of colored patterns to resemble a patchwork quilt. Four panels of fret-cut wood, two at the front and two at the sides, were backed with textured amber-colored glass; lit from behind, these gave off the same glow and color as candlelight. The metalwork on the cabinet, finished in an antique

A 1940 article in a US trade magazine sought rather desperately to boost the operators' morale:

> It isn't beyond the memory of any of us, that a person connected with the coin machine industry was generally looked upon as something that just crawled out of a log. Today, your neighbor sees in you a man who is his social equal – not someone to be avoided. He recognizes you as an integral part of an industry that is contributing greatly to this nation's wealth and knowledge. He knows now that your business is an important one. And a rapidly growing one. He knows too that the coin machine industry in all its component parts – manufacturing, distributing and operating – not only affords employment to tens of thousands, but gives recreation, relaxation and enjoyment to millions more! [Dan Hawley, *Coin Machine Journal*, August 1940.]

Perhaps with the new generation of bright, luxurious machines this was the right time to dissociate the industry from its past, to make a new start. It was suggested that maybe dropping the name "jukebox" (which the manufacturers themselves had never favored) could help. We can cite a typical trade-press article of the time among the many which supported this view:

With the daily press raining such words as "jukeboxes," "slot machines" and "coin-in-the-slot" machines upon an industry that is trying to clear its skirts of unfavorable comment by the general public, operators, distributors and manufacturers are currently noted to be rising up against the use of abbreviated and slang words in their general conversations and in the press of the industry.

As one operator expressed it, "Why should we continue to talk slang out of the sides of our mouths when now is the best time we've ever had to improve our good name in the eyes of the general public?" Although the matter may be regarded by some as a minor blemish on the industry, if all in the coin machine business would take it upon themselves to make a better impression, the words "coin machine" soon would not be immediately connected in the mind of the public with "hoodlums." [*Coin Machine Journal*, August 1940.]

"Automatic phonographs" was the favored euphemism, but in fact the public naturally preferred the name by which they already knew these machines: "jukeboxes." And never was there a time when jukeboxes were as "jukeboxy" as they were in the early 1940s.

The ultimate jukebox of the decade in terms of opulence was the magnificent 1941 Wurlitzer Model 850, the "Peacock." The Wurlitzer brochure talked of "sure-fire showmanship" and, with the slogan "you're a showman too – give the public something new," drew an analogy between a theater changing its program to maintain public interest and an operator keeping a site alive with new models. In case of any lingering doubt in the operator's mind about being able to afford to keep up with the apparently endless fertility of Paul Fuller's imagination and Wurlitzer's manufacturing ability, the whole thing was spelled out in detail:

> Music merchants know that you can't leave the same phonograph in the same location year after year and expect maximum profits . . . they move their older phonographs right down the line to their second, third and fourth class spots – giving every location a newer Wurlitzer every year . . . you'll realize that the cardinal rule of all show business – "change the show to draw the crowd" – applies to your business too.

This idea, while hardly new, did not always work out, and the ploy was probably the reason why many operators rejected the Model 780: the more a jukebox is designed with one sort of site in mind, the more difficult it is for people to assimilate it into another. Also, it occasionally happened that the people in a particular locality would, unaccountably, "adopt" a jukebox – developing a liking for it and resisting any attempt on the operator's part to move it on, or protesting strongly if they found it had suddenly been replaced.

Irrespective of the commercial aspects, the concept of showmanship was the key to Wurlitzer's design philosophy. Its mastery at packaging the jukebox as a piece of visual excitement was more essential to its image than any technological development: this was a weakness which, at the end of the decade, would be responsible for Wurlitzer's loss of market supremacy. But in 1941 the biggest, the showiest, the most "jukeboxy" of all jukeboxes was the Wurlitzer Model 850. In terms of the shape of the cabinet it was basically just a very large Model 750, and like the 750 it had back-colored plastics: in the 850, however, rather than the glow of the illuminated plastics extending the apparent size of the box the opposite effect was created, a soft halo of color framing the front. As in the Model 800, the top sides were almost completely taken up by large illuminated plastic panels, linked with elaborate – and unfortunately fragile – scrolls of cast metal.

Nothing was allowed to distract the eye from the center of the jukebox, which constituted the example *par excellence* of Wurlitzer's "romantic" period. Framed in rich walnut was a shield of glass with two peacocks screened onto it – an evocative image, reminiscent more of the 1920s than of the 1940s, and set against a deep azure background. The peacocks were translucent and lit from behind. But not merely lit: the magic of the peacock glass, which mystified those who first saw it, lay in its unique use of polarized light. A system of chain-driven polarizing discs broke up the light to create an effect of ever-changing iridescence. Neither before nor since has there ever been a jukebox quite so theatrical.

The peacocks were absolutely distinctive: they could not have been made by anyone else. They were surrounded by the simple yet beautiful metal grille, which curved up on either side and was surmounted

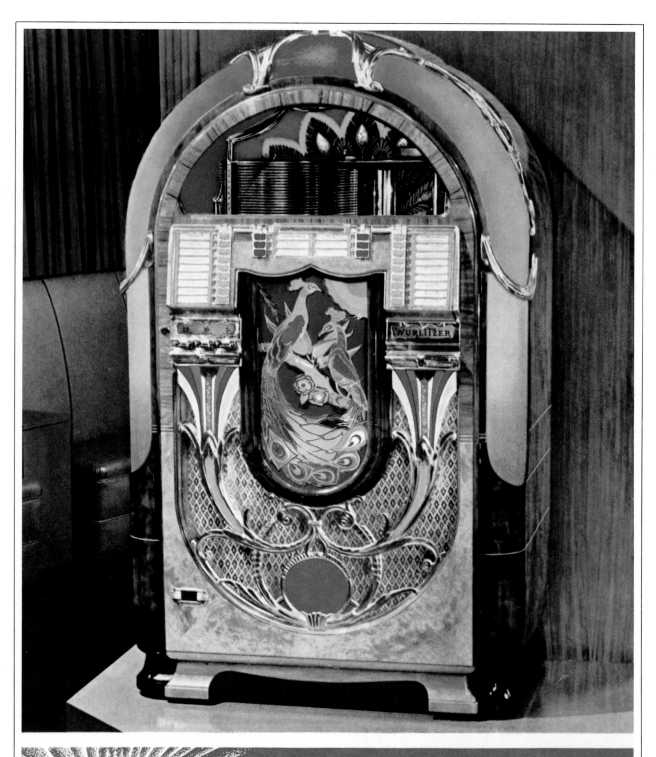

by fans or fountains of light in a style similar to that used on the Model 750. On either side of the peacocks were two metal castings. One housed the coin slides and denomination plate – which, back-lit, glowed a soft yellow. The other had a matching window which simply read "Wurlitzer."

The Model 850 was to be Wurlitzer's last full-scale production jukebox before the United States entered World War II. The last few 850s were modified to become the 850A. The major difference here was that the peacock glass was replaced with one depicting stylized flowers against a dark background. This machine did not have a polarizing unit: instead, the stems of the flowers were bubble tubes.

The "tulip" panel was incorporated also in a stunning wallbox/remote speaker combination, the Model 580. About the same size as a small jukebox, this wall-mounted unit used the minimum of metal in its construction. Although the United States was not yet at war, the use of metal in nonessentials was already restricted.

The 1941 Model 780 was still being advertised in 1942 as a continued line; however, with jukeboxes as with other consumer items, "held over" is usually a euphemistic way of saying that the manufacturer still has some old stock left. In any event, people wishing to buy the last new model available before World War II put an end to production were placing their orders for the "Victory" Model 950.

The contrast with the "Peacock" was dramatic. It is almost as if, anticipating the outbreak of war, Fuller had enjoyed a final fling when designing it. At this stage, in creative terms, he had the world at his feet: he had his own private enclave at the Wurlitzer factory, where he and his design team worked without interference, and the company was more than ready to provide the money and manufacturing skills necessary for his visions to be turned into reality. Now, largely deprived of two of the materials – plastic and metal – which he had hitherto deployed in such a flamboyant manner, he showed his true mas-

ABOVE *The somber beauty of the Model 850A is echoed in the 580 selector speaker.*

tery. Unlike the Model 780, the 950 was no pastiche: it was very visibly a jukebox. Frugally making the best use of the small quantities of metal and plastic he was allowed to use on the cabinet, Fuller created a beautiful, original masterpiece. There is perhaps a touch of sadness in the 950's beauty, lacking as it does the glitter of nickel: one might say whimsically that it reflects the somber mood of a nation preparing for war. Arch-topped, the machine has proportions suggesting height and narrowness; large round wooden feet, painted black, lead upward into ribbed wooden columns which are then stepped inward to harmonize with the tall outer pilasters. These pilasters (plastic on some machines, glass on others) were molded in a series of half rounds, back-painted white but with their strips left clear. Through the strips could be seen the bubble tubes, running the whole way up the pilasters and illuminated fluorescently. The pilasters met at the top with heavily molded pilaster caps ("shoulders") pierced by a narrow strip of amber plastic which emitted a shaft of golden light. The

RIGHT *Views of the massive Wurlitzer factory in Montreal, Canada.*

WURLITZER'S THE WINNER WITH *A Name Famous in Music for over Two Hundred Years*

There is every reason why Wurlitzer's The Winner in beauty, tone and mechanical perfection.

The name "Wurlitzer" has been associated with fine musical instruments for over 200 years. Wurlitzer's experience is equalled by no other company in the coin machine industry.

It is not by chance that 70% of all Music Merchants choose Wurlitzer Automatic Phonographs or that there are more Wurlitzers on location today than all other makes combined. It's a direct result of an established fact — Wurlitzers get and hold the best locations — make the most money!

The Rudolph Wurlitzer Company, North Tonawanda, N. Y. Canadian Factory: RCA-Victor Co., Ltd., Montreal, Quebec, Canada.

Wurlitzer combed the country to build its engineering staff. It is composed entirely of specialists whose training and experience qualifies them for their particular type of work.

Wurlitzer operates the world's largest plant devoted exclusively to manufacturing automatic phonographs and other musical instruments. Its equipment and facilities are the finest in the automatic music industry.

Wurlitzer's thorough testing and inspection methods are directly responsible for the accurate assembly and rugged quality that marks all Wurlitzer models — makes them first choice of Music Merchants.

Wurlitzer Automatic Phonographs Are SOLD ONLY TO MUSIC MERCHANTS

Cigar stores, General stores, Beauty Parlors, Lodge Rooms, Bus Terminals.

DRUG STORES

Ice Cream and Candy Stores, Airports, Hotels, Country Clubs, Billiard Parlors.

SODA PARLORS

Small Bars, Cocktail Lounges, Barber Shops, Tourist Camps, Filling Stations.

MILK BARS

Diners, Roadside Stands, Counter-type Restaurants, Chinese Restaurants.

LUNCH ROOMS

ABOVE *Although Rock-Ola and some minor companies produced countertops, Wurlitzer's success in the marketplace was assured by Paul Fuller's designs.*

nature of these caps indicates the economies made in the construction of the 950: on some machines they are in hand-carved wood, with various scraps being bonded together to make the blocks from which the pieces were carved; others were constructed from plaster. In both instances they were stained a very dark brown to disguise the materials used.

The machine was topped with a crown casting in the form of "Prince of Wales" feathers; these were made in the same way as the pilaster caps. The arch itself comprised two panels of printed plastic, depicting Pan playing his pipes. The "deer glass" of the front door was, like these, very much an Art Deco image. The leaping deer, flanking the grille, changed color as the cylinder in the pilasters revolved.

It is ironic that the Model 950, made in such adverse circumstances, is now regarded as one of Paul Fuller's finest creations and one of the loveliest juke-

LEFT *A triumph of Paul Fuller's design expertise over the shortage of materials, the Model 950 was the last pre-war Wurlitzer.*

boxes of all time. It represented the end of the pre-war "Wurlitzer years." In a moment we shall discuss Wurlitzer's wartime production, but first let us step back a few years to look at Wurlitzer's "doll's-house" jukeboxes, the countertop models.

These mini-jukeboxes were originally introduced by Wurlitzer in 1937 (Model 51); indeed, only Rock-Ola among the other manufacturers ever made countertops, issuing two models in 1939 and 1940. As was to be expected, it was Paul Fuller who turned these little machines from utility items into art objects. The whole idea of the countertop jukebox was to gain access to sites where space precluded a full-size machine, and by their very nature these sites tended to be at the lower end of the market – ice-cream parlors, milk bars and soda fountains. Nevertheless, Wurlitzer's marketing was determined not to miss *any* opportunities there might be to place a machine. The fact that between 1939 and 1942 it produced nearly 16,000 countertops shows both the strength of its determination and the success of the idea.

WURLITZER's THE WINNER with

Model 41

THE SMALLEST AUTOMATIC PHONOGRAPH EVER BUILT

EACH IS A

Complete Phonograph

WITH A

Built-In Speaker

● Another Wurlitzer triumph! Smallest automatic phonograph ever built yet it sparkles with big phonograph features! Glamour Lighting! Cabinet finished four sides! Visible Record Changer and Mechanical Record Selector! Wide Range Adjustable Tone! Hi-Speed Service Set-Up! ● This brilliant little beauty plays 12 records — is furnished with Magnetic Coin Equipment — can be easily carried into any location. An excellent testing model to prove, in advance, profits that might be expected from installation of a larger Wurlitzer. ● Think of the profit possibilities in soda parlors, lunch cars, counter-type restaurants, bars, cocktail lounges — on the bar of locations that also have a larger phonograph! The Wurlitzer Counter Model 41 costs so little to buy and to operate — it's a guaranteed big money maker.

Two Sensational New Counter Models

Model 71

A COUNTER MODEL PHONOGRAPH WITH CONSOLE MODEL FEATURES

● Here is a Counter Model Phonograph alive with Console Model features. Sensational play appeal. Cabinet finished on four sides. Piano-type keyboard. Wide Range Adjustable Tone that accurately reproduces every instrument in the orchestra. ● Longer record and needle life through important improvements in pick-up and tone arm design. Elimination of butterfly switches by Wurlitzer's revolutionary Moto-Drive Coin Switch. 5—10—25 cent Magnetic Coin Equipment. Mechanical Record Selector. Standard Play Meter. ● New Hi-Speed Service Set-Up offering amazing accessibility of all parts for quick, economical servicing. See the "Seventy One" in action. You'll marvel at its glorious Glamour Lighting. Hear it play and you'll say, "Wurlitzer's The Winner in the Counter Model field."

BOTH HAVE

Glamour Lighting

AND

Visible Record Changers

ABOVE *"Converting an old Wurlitzer into a modernized Wurlitzer is a money-making move." An estimated 18,000 "Victory" conversions were used to substitute for the lack of new machines during World War II.*

Aggressive marketing alone, however, could not have produced sales figures like these: the jukeboxes themselves were largely responsible. Designed to stand on counters or on specially constructed stands, which ranged from the strictly functional to the luxurious, these little machines had to capture all the glamour and quality associated with the name of Wurlitzer. With a perfect sense of scale, Fuller designed them to *complement* the full-size jukeboxes rather than to be smaller, less elaborate versions.

The most beautiful were undoubtedly models 71 and 81. Introduced in 1940 as a deluxe model, the 71

used curved plastics and a petite decorative metal grille to give it an air of luxury. Its successor, the 81, was identical save that here the plastic had a colored marble effect.

Even had the entry of the United States into World War II not obviated further production, it is unlikely that more countertops would have been made. They were right for their time, but they depended for much of their success on their novelty value. Much later, in the 1950s, Rock-Ola launched a modern equivalent of the countertop, but mini-jukeboxes were never again to be of any significance.

The rationing of materials which had come into effect in 1941 became a total ban by the spring of 1942. Paul Fuller had achieved wonders with the Model 950 (whose mechanism sported a wooden tone-arm pillar because of the shortage of metal!), but the supply of mechanisms was exhausted; ironically, the demand for jukeboxes was set to be greater than ever. The quality of Wurlitzer's construction insured that there were plenty of serviceable old machines around, but clearly it was not in the company's interest to have these back on site. How could they overcome this problem – no metal, no plastics, no manufacturing capacity and, uh, no *mechanism*? Paul Fuller (who must have thought back with nostalgia to the

---

BELOW The "modernized" wartime versions, the "Victory" models, kept the name Wurlitzer alive and helped pave the way for the company's post-war success.

heady "Peacock" days) once again came up with an answer – an empty cabinet into which old mechanisms could be introduced. Created from scraps of wood by craftsmen who had in many instances been brought out of retirement, the cabinet necessarily lacked the usual curves; one constraint was that glass had to be used where there would normally have been plastic.

1942's "Victory," despite all these limitations, conveys a typical Wurlitzer air of luxury and authority. The sharply angled cabinet is sometimes referred to as the "coffin," but those angles were necessary to give the cabinet some degree of strength. Flanked by two massive ornate pedestals, made of wood and plaster but looking as if they were carved out of solid ebony and strong enough to support a cathedral, the flat wooden front, pierced with a grille screen incorporating Model 950's feather motif, had at its top a circular door. Half of this door was the mechanism window. The bottom half varied from machine to machine, because the "Victory" was designed as a "universal" cabinet which could be used to update older Wurlitzers: some required an aperture for a "rotary" selector and others for a keyboard.

This idea of a "universal" cabinet was, of course, not new: as we have seen, there was a spate of them produced in the late 1930s and early 1940s as a way of updating old-fashioned, pre-light-up machines. However, as with all the machines Paul Fuller created, there is a special "presence" about the "Victory" which, despite the conditions under which the jukebox was made, distinguishes it. The side panels show on the left a pierrot and on the right the lady whom he is serenading. Just like the pierrot the "Victory" wore a strange costume and brought music to millions. Approximately 18,000 of these "Victory" conversions were made between 1942 and 1945, and the continuing presence of "new" Wurlitzers throughout the war years did much to keep the company's image at the forefront of public awareness and pave the way for its post-war success.

3 LET THE JUKEBOX KEEP ON PLAYING

In 1942 the jukebox manufacturers faced not only the loss of their manufacturing wings to the war industry (where their contribution was recognized as outstanding) and the departure of key personnel, from service engineers to secretaries, either to join the armed services or to do other essential war work: they had to cope with a threat from their very life source, the musicians themselves. The President of the American Federation of Musicians, James Caesar Petrillo, had an almost pathological hatred of jukeboxes. He had seen thousands of musicians thrown out of work with the advent of Prohibition, only to find on repeal that their places had been usurped by the jukebox. Petrillo, a larger-than-life character whose armored car and bodyguards alone at one stage cost his members $25,000 a year, declared war on the machines. A contemporary article explained:

Over the years, Petrillo's stubbornest obstacle has been so-called canned music. There are some 350,000 jukeboxes in operation in the United States and he despises each and every one of them. "Icemen are losing their jobs to Frigidaires the same way that a lot of musicians are losing their jobs to canned music. But there's a difference: the iceman doesn't have anything to do with the machine that robs him of a job, whereas the musician does 'manufacture' the recorded music that is played over and over on radio and in those nickel-record machines thousands of times to rob other musicians of a chance to work." His hatred for the jukebox has all the aspects of a highly personal vendetta and he speaks of the machines as if they were animate. "Them damn t'ings!" he shouts. "Everybody gets a slice of that juke money, the machine maker, the man who rents it, the song writer, but the musician gets nothing except what he was paid for the original single recording. His record keeps some little band from getting a job in a roadhouse or a restaurant." [George Frazier, *Collier's Magazine*, March 1947.]

LEFT AND ABOVE *Seeburg concentrated on the idea of a complete music system, of which the key feature was the "wireless" wall box.*

Petrillo had a point, but his was only a partial story. One of the reasons for the popularity of the jukebox was the increasing public awareness of music through radios and records.

However, that "little band" could not bring the sounds of Artie Shaw or Glenn Miller to a cocktail bar, but the jukebox could. A 1940 article summed things up:

> By this time radio had made America music-conscious. The demand for economical, unusual entertainment surged forcefully as a result of the depressing early 1930s. Coin-operated phonographs made their appearance first in somber dress with nothing of "eye appeal" except newness and nothing of "ear appeal" except musical reproduction. Eventually the coin-operated phonograph field was revolutionized. An entirely new type of music vendor appeared in restaurants, tearooms and amusement spots. Startling improvement in sound and appearance quickly made the coin-operated phonograph business a highly important industry. The popularity of phonographs has also been aided by the radio. It is this continuous world of music for the average person that is rapidly developing over 100,000,000 American adults into music critics. Coin-operated phonographs, through a tremendously wide distribution, appeal to millions of individuals every day, thus insuring for this industry an important part in the next phase of American music. [Jack Nelson, *Billboard*, June 1940.]

Others joined to defend the jukebox against Petrillo's rantings. The music publishers decided that it was an ally in "popularizing music." *Billboard* quoted Jack Robbins, the music publisher, as saying, "This medium of music exploitation . . . will afford a better 'buying gauge' to music publishers." The article continued:

ABOVE *The "Wall-o-matic" brought music selection to the table.*

It is Robbins' contention that if a person will spend five cents to hear a song, other people will spend thirty-five cents to play it from a sheet music copy.

In paying tribute to the importance of the music box Robbins points out: "If a song is spotted in only 100,000 machines, or 25 per cent of the total available, and was played only once a night to an average listening audience of five people, that would be a half-million 'hearing units' of performances. But we know that a song gets from three to six plays a night, and so we can depend upon a few million 'hearing units' in a period of two or three weeks." [*Billboard*, June 1940.]

Still, nothing would deter Petrillo from his quest to destroy the hated jukebox. In 1942 he succeeded in achieving a total ban on all new recordings. President Roosevelt himself attempted to get the ban lifted, arguing that recorded music (and, by implication, the jukebox) was an essential morale-booster in wartime. For nearly two years no new records were made, until an agreement was reached whereby the musicians would receive a royalty of 1 per cent of the retail price of every record made. The strike was the biggest of all organized threats to the jukebox, but by this time the machine had become too established a part of US popular culture to be at risk of extinction.

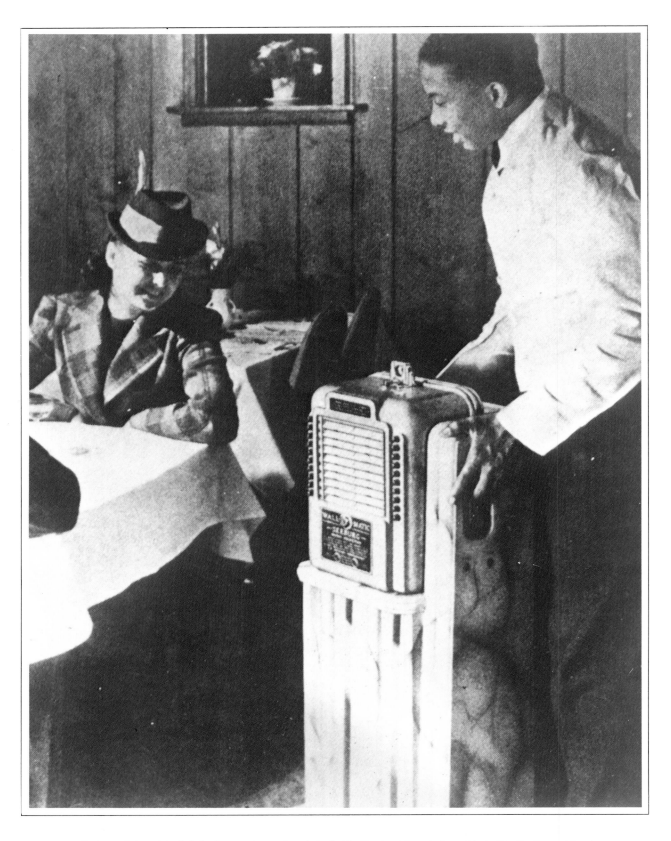

ABOVE *Seeburg originated the "wireless" system (soon adopted also by Wurlitzer) which made it possible the "stroller," or mobile selector.*

42

ABOVE *An unusual sales ploy. One of Rock-Ola's distributors in Texas mounted his company's 1940 "Super Luxury Light-up" and "dial-a-tune" wall box onto the back of his automobile.*

As we have seen, much of the credit for the public's enthusiasm for the jukebox must go to Wurlitzer, with its constant introduction of stimulating new models and its emphasis on glamour. Yet it is far from the case that Wurlitzer was close to achieving a monopoly. Its main competitors were Seeburg and Rock-Ola, the former being the more important.

Seeburg's products, in comparison with Wurlitzer's offerings, seemed almost puritanical. The emphasis was on solid engineering. This was because the company's mainstream production was of a vast array of non-jukebox items, ranging from automatic vendors to electronic devices. The development of the light-up cabinet in 1938 had established Seeburg as a major force in the jukebox industry, but it was the company's introduction of the Seeburg "music system" that really brought it to the fore. The idea of wall boxes, or remote selector units, was by no means new: they had existed even in the old days of orchestrions, as simple coin-collectors. Seeburg's concept was that remote selector units would pull extra

nickels from the pockets of patrons too engrossed in their conversation or their meal to want to get up and walk over to the jukebox. Aside from this marketing factor, there were two further motivations. First, there was the simple fact that the technology was now available. Second, from 1938 onward Seeburg enclosed its mechanism; although its cabinet design was very stylish, there was nothing in particular to entice the patron to the jukebox.

The earliest wall boxes were multi-wire (each selection required a separate wire linked to the jukebox), but Seeburg almost immediately brought out a "wireless" system, whereby the selections could be programmed using pulses sent along the location's existing electrical wiring. This enabled Seeburg to develop the "lazy jukebox" to its logical conclusion – the "play-boy" or "stroller," a wall box housed in a cabinet which could be wheeled up to the patron.

Although Wurlitzer and Rock-Ola likewise brought out wall-box systems in 1940 (as did smaller manufacturers, such as the Buckley Company, which offered a universal wall box which could be linked to any make of jukebox), it was Seeburg's commitment to a complete music system which established its preeminence in the field, and was later to be responsible for the fact that the wall box – usually a Seeburg unit – became a key feature of diner art."

At the same time Rock-Ola was developing a remote system to rival Seeburg's. It, too, had decided on a covered mechanism for the 1940s and, although its jukeboxes were fancier than Seeburg's, with "marble" plastics and decorative metal – something Seeburg never went in for – the motivations were much the same. Rock-Ola actually claimed that "carefully conducted national surveys prove that greater ornateness in phonograph design can only serve to increase the price of equipment to the operator without commensurately increasing his profits."

The Rock-Ola wall box and bar box had an additional novelty: the telephone-dial selector. The "dial-

ABOVE *The massive "Spectravox" was actually no more than a selector system and speaker for the "Playmaster" hideaway.*

a-tune," was also incorporated in the 1941 "Spectra-vox." This was an amazing device – a free-standing selector unit and speaker. It was designed to link up either with a Rock-Ola jukebox (Model 1801) or with a "hideaway" (Model 1802). The hideaway was a jukebox without coin equipment and was, as the name implies, tucked away under the bar or in the basement. The "Spectravox" was not entirely original – AMI had already produced a free-standing "tower" speaker – but Rock-Ola developed the idea into a massive (nearly 7ft high!) and rather beautiful decor item. Standing on a metal Art Deco-style base was a wooden cabinet whose proportions suggested that it may originally have been designed to contain the changer mechanism. Rising up from this was an illuminated metal column housing the "dial-a-tune" selector, title strips and coin entry. The "Spectravox" was topped by the speaker bowl, which was reminiscent of the uplighter lampshades of the 1930s. The

bowl, it was claimed, projected the music better than a conventional speaker could in that it bounced it off the ceiling, so bringing out the entire spectrum of sound – hence the name "Spectravox." A smaller version, without the selector mechanism and the bowl, was available as an extension speaker.

The selector and the coin system of the "Spectra-vox" were married to the "Playmaster" hideaway unit to create Rock-Ola's last pre-war jukeboxes, 1942's "Premier," "President" and "Commando." These juke-boxes were restricted by the lack of metal and plastic: aside from the bottom, all the panels had to be made of glass. As designs, the three machines owe every-thing to the earlier light-up consoles of 1940 and 1941. Although they were considerably taller – just over 6ft high – their scale was better suited to the round-shouldered illuminated panels.

Nevertheless, although the ideas of top-emitted sound and the "tone column" were good ones, and at least in theory correct, the sheer height of these machines surely limited their application. Rock-Ola is generally regarded as a rather conservative com-pany which has usually fought shy of innovation: it is therefore particularly curious that this range of machines should be among the most original and unconventional of any in jukebox history.

BELOW *The Rock-Ola "dial-a-tune" wall box from 1940.*

ABOVE *The "Spectravox" and "Playmaster" were combined for the "Premier," "President" and "Commando" models. Illustrated is the "Commando."*

AMI, which had enjoyed limited success with "Singing Towers," during the 1940s almost retired from jukebox production to concentrate instead on its "Automatic Hostess" telephone system. This simple system, first introduced in 1939, was an attempt to bypass the limitations of the jukebox. The site was linked *via* a coin-operated microphone to a central station where disc jockeys operated banks of turntables in order to play the record back to the site. Both the human element and the much larger selection of records were claimed as advantages over the jukebox:

> When you operate the Hostess you are dealing directly in human personality, in the convincing and pleasing sound of the feminine voice, in the fantasy of the Hostess personality which at one and the same time is as intimate as one of your own family and as remote as an angel in heaven. The Automatic Hostess is everything a phonograph is and much more. It is a phonograph with personality plus, and along with this personality goes the richness of offering thousands of music selections where only a few dozen were possible before.

Not only had the Hostess the "voice of an angel," she was obliging, too!

> For ten cents she'll announce that the tune is dedicated to a friend right in the location. For twenty-five cents she'll announce and play a special tune in another Hostess location on the same circuit where the friend will be astonished and tremendously pleased by this salute.

Rock-Ola introduced a similar system in 1941, "Mystic Music." However, it promoted this less as an alternative to the jukebox than as an additional feature. The conventional jukebox was modified to serve as a "Mystic Music" station, although the two could not

ABOVE *AMI resumed the telephone music system at the end of World War II. Here is the 1947 "Automatic Hostess."*

be in use at the same time: "By simply throwing a concealed switch on the side of the phonograph, the location owner gives his patrons conventional music or Mystic Music, whichever they prefer." Like the AMI system, this one was doomed, because in 1942 the nation was at war, and the "angel-voiced" hostesses went off to become switchboard operators for military centers or industrial installations, or to take on other wartime tasks.

Neither Wurlitzer nor Seeburg got involved in the telephone music business. Wurlitzer had taken as gospel Capehart's comment that 24 selections were all the public would ever want, and seemed to be developing its machines on the basis that the jukebox itself was as much the entertainment as the music. Seeburg, meanwhile, had been casting a critical eye over the scene, and had come to the conclusion that, in its present form, the jukebox was too limited to be capable of sustained progress. In 1941 Seeburg initiated the development that, by the end of the decade, would revolutionize the jukebox. At the same time, Seeburg had negotiated several military contracts,

ABOVE *Operators were urged to help keep their jukeboxes in action throughout the war – a patriotic appeal!*

and so it is possible that it regarded its pre-war models as little more than a stopgap.

Even so, the Seeburgs of this period were stylistically important. The four 1940 models (the "Cadet," "Colonel," "Commander" and "Concert Master") followed the same lines as 1939's "Classic" and "Vogue." Unlike Wurlitzer, which was like a quick-change artist parading various models in an ever-altering array of cabinet styles and moods, Seeburg was content to ring the changes on the house style it had already established. The acoustic properties of the cabinet (to which Wurlitzer seemed indifferent) were essential to the rich tone reproduction characteristic of Seeburg machines. Consequently, the bottom half of the cabinet remained the same, with a broad speaker-screen area protected by a center column (or, in the case of the 1941 model, two columns); the column was back-illuminated to give a rich glow to the speaker screen without interfering with the trans-

mission of sound. The casters on which the machine moved were hidden behind a solid, contoured bottom skirt, imparting the impression that the heavy-looking machine rested directly on the floor. Emphasizing this "substantial" appearance, the illuminated plastic panels were in a deep red and seemed as solid as the rest of the cabinet. Nothing bubbled, flickered or changed color, and no fancy metal distracted from the classic lines. These monumental machines had nothing lighthearted about them; on the other hand, nothing could equal their sound.

For the 1941 Seeburg models – the "Hi Tones" – moving light was introduced and the conventional grille area had disappeared. These bizarre-looking machines – known as "turrets" or "cotton reels" and looking like two-stepped flat-backed cylinders, one on top of the other – had their speaker at the top so that, as with a "Spectravox," the sound was thrown upward and outward; the whole top section was in effect the speaker enclosure. This meant that the designers were free to enhance the bottom section, which housed the mechanism, with illumination. Set in the rich and solid-looking wood of the cabinet, the center was taken up with a faceted panel through which shone the "fountain of light" (i.e., the moving lights). Either side of this, a pair of greenish amber panels glowed. For the 1942 "Hi Tone" model these panels were replaced by glass ones.

As with all 1942 models, production of these was limited as the manufacturers, one by one, shut down their jukebox capacity in order to concentrate on the war effort. It was the end of an era.

BELOW *Seeburg's 1941 "Hi Tone Super," Model 8800.*

4 A NICKEL'S WORTH OF FUN

When the United States emerged from World War II, few could have imagined that the nation could pick up where it had left off. A contemporary magazine article summed it up as "a fidgety interim between two orders, with yesterday's security quivering before a new unpredictable age" [Robert C Ruark, *Collier's Magazine*, December 1946]. The same article refers to the "fouled-up forties" and, in the midst of an appraisal of the social and economic confusion of the time, to the adjustment to peacetime roles:

> . . . the garage mechanic was a marine on Bougainville. The milkman was the only survivor of his platoon at Cassino. The doctor was at Bastogne; the grocer was a supply sergeant on Tinian; the cab-driver pushed a B-29 from Guam to Honshu, and the lawyer packed a dagger for the office of strategic services . . .

It examines also the effect on those not directly involved in the war, in this instance the bobby-soxers:

> The bobby-soxer is a product of wartime stress. When the draft was shuttling her male contemporary into uniform, the teenaged girl spent her emotions on a few draft-exempt symbols like Frank Sinatra and other warty-voiced baritones. Inchoate emotions were transferred to voices which mooed gently from jukeboxes.

The writer was obviously not a Sinatra fan! Nevertheless, the general point was a valid one. Jukeboxes had, during the war years, established themselves at home and abroad as a major form of entertainment and, by its very nature, listening to a jukebox is both a public and a private experience. The music fills the room, hopefully to be enjoyed by everyone in a shared experience, yet for one person in that room – the person who selected the number – the machine is playing "their" song.

ABOVE *The enduring image of Wurlitzer's Model 1015 spans from the Wright Morris photograph* Jukebox, Southern Indiana, 1950 *to today's cans of the famous "Rock & Roll" beer.*

Today we can feel empathy with those wartime teenagers – indeed, we may sometime or other ourselves have been one of the thousands of men and women who have entered that private world where the jukebox seems intimate, playing just for us. And the jukebox brightest in most people's memories and which inspires the most nostalgia has to be the Wurlitzer Model 1015.

One of the reasons why the 1015 was the paramount jukebox is that it never really went away. Right up to the late 1950s you could still find second-hand models advertised in the trade papers – at prices that would make present-day collectors and dealers weep! It was to be found on location, usually converted to 45rpm, all through the rock'n'roll years – so much so that many people think of it as a 1950s machine. Moreover, not long after they had ceased to be of any

RIGHT *This present-day illustration captures the feeling of the 1940s, linking two cult figures of the day – Betty Grable and Wurlitzer's 1015.*

commercial use these Wurlitzers were "rediscovered." They were used in artwork for rock'n'roll albums, sought out and refurbished by enthusiasts who wanted to keep a piece of history, kept *alive* – in other words, it feels as if this jukebox never disappeared, that it just slept for a few years.

Why did the Model 1015 become the cult classic, the very symbol of the jukebox? Well, partly it was because so many were made – the generally accepted figure is 56,000 – partly because it had a very good design (simple, easily recognized lines and yet plenty of jukebox "flash"), and partly because Wurlitzer, for the first time in jukebox history, ran a massive publicity campaign to promote it.

Normally jukebox advertising is directed at the operators, those actually buying the product. But Wurlitzer had always been part of the public consciousness: everyone knew of its movie-theater organs – the "Mighty Wurlitzers" – and of its pianos, home organs, even radios. During the war years the name had been kept alive, through the 1942 "Victory" model and advertising. The publicity campaign for the 1015 (and, to a much lesser extent, for the Model 1080 and Model 1100) was aimed at the end consumer. A series of ads featuring full-page colorful illustrations appeared in the popular magazines – *Collier's*, the *Saturday Evening Post*, *Life*, *Better Homes and Gardens*, and so on. These created the image of the Wurlitzer as an integral part of "the American way of life." The seasons and festivals – Christmas, Easter, summer vacations, Halloween, Thanksgiving and all – were marked by advertisements showing the Wurlitzer as the focus of an appropriate social gathering. Then there were other events to be enhanced by the Wurlitzer: the birthday party, the wedding reception, the meal out, the snack lunch at a roadside inn and so on. All painted by the same artist, Albert Dorne, these tableaux captured a mood of the 1940s – relaxed, companionable and affluent –

RIGHT *Wurlitzer's billboard art was seen along the highways.*

The Waltz She Will Always Remember

Musical Fun for Everyone

Stop— Linger and Listen!

Musical Fun for Everyone

24 Top Bands Played at Her Party

Musical Fun for Everyone

Only two waitresses

...yet 24 of America's top bands play here every day

America's favorite nickel's worth of fun

LEFT AND ABOVE *Various advertisements from the popular magazines of the time demonstrated the ubiquity of the jukebox.*

ABOVE *Wurlitzer's logo, affectionately known as "Johnny-one-note," appeared everywhere and on everything: (from left to right) a Wurlitzer decal would be affixed to the windows of bars and restaurants to announce that there was "Wurlitzer music" inside; "Johnny-one-note" swizzle stick; Wurlitzer operator's card; a drinks coaster and a menu from 1946.*

with which many North Americans could identify.

Each advertisement carried the new Wurlitzer logo, a top-hatted musical note playing the trumpet. It was officially called the "Sign of the Musical Note" but commonly known as "Johnny-one-note," and sites were encouraged to display it. "The Sign of the Musical Note identifies places where you can have fun playing a Wurlitzer," read the advertisements; by implication, inside was a happy crowd, just like in the ads – all you had to do was walk in and join them.

At the time no other company of any sort was conducting such a sustained and varied campaign. The press advertisements were reinforced by billboard art. Catchy phrases drove the message home – "America's Favorite Nickel's Worth of Fun," "Musical Fun for Everyone," "The Name That Means Music to Millions" and "America's Favorite Musical Pastime." Every chance to exploit the name was taken. Sites were equipped with Wurlitzer napkins, drinks coasters, menus and swizzle sticks. Operators were provided with cards bearing the logo, and they could have these printed up as business cards.

The Wurlitzer ads created an image. In the public mind the name "Wurlitzer" was synonymous with the word "jukebox," and the jukebox was, of course, part of "the American way of life" – to the extent that in a

1946 letter a concerned Australian expressed his fears quite strongly:

Apart from the necessities of pre-war civilization, we in Australia lack some of the higher refinements of postwar America described in *Life* [magazine]. Jukeboxes . . . nylon stockings, emancipation of "teenagers" and central heating as an obvious item of domestic equipment are some of the things which we can look forward to, though our feelings may not be entirely in the nature of fulsome welcome when they do reach here. Personally, I think that if the invention of the jukebox had been quietly strangled at birth the peace-loving world would have suffered no irreparable loss. As for the emancipation of "teenagers," though there is undoubtedly some good in the notion that youth must have its fling, I cannot see any reason why college girls should adopt as uniform men's trousers rolled up to the knee and men's shirt-tails flapping daintily behind. Nor can I see any future in the habits of Californian boys whose hobby is speeding across the California sands in "hopped-up" jalopies. That is, I cannot see any future in the pastime unless California is over-populated . . . [*Life Magazine*, 1946].

ABOVE *In this tongue-in-cheek illustration* Life Magazine *summed up the jukebox and hot-rod culture that some foreigners saw as symptomatic of late-1940s North America.*

The Model 1015 itself was not a new design (a fact Wurlitzer itself tacitly acknowledged when it later advertised the Model 1100 as the first real post-war jukebox). Looking back to the Model 950, we can see that the basic shape was already established in 1942. We can speculate that, had there not been the limitations imposed by the imminence of war, the 950 would have had at least a metal top-crown casting and probably a metal grille as well. Look at a 1015 with half-closed eyes and you will see the ghost of a 950!

In its finished form, the 1015 was almost a symbol of the speed at which the United States had recommenced peacetime production. The cabinet had bright nickel-plated castings all over and a magnificently styled grille with deep arabesque scrolls at the base leading into an open lattice pattern; the diamond design of the grille was echoed in the small diamonds of the cream-and-gold weave of the speaker cloth. Bubble tubes enlivened the almost unbroken archway of plastic, the lower pilasters diffusing the light from colored turning cylinders (which also glowed through the inner grille surround), resulting in an ever-changing sequence of saccharin-sweet color. The top arch glowed a warm pale amber – or, in some instances, "tri-color" plastics, with three bands of diffused color, added another dimension. The center of the arch featured nickel "feather" cast-

ings, between which glowed a panel of bright-red plastic; these were the climax of the evolution of a feature that went right back through the 950, 850, 750, 800 and 700 series.

There were other references to the past. The style of the side castings, which joined the upper curves to the pilaster plastics, was derived from those used on the 500 and 600 models. The bottom of the front grille was reminiscent of the scroll castings of the Model 850. In effect, the Model 1015 in many ways represented a summary of what had gone before, harmonizing the various experiences of the "Wurlitzer Years" in order to create the definitive Wurlitzer. A new age had arrived, and the decorative 1930s, upon which much of Paul Fuller's design concepts had been based, suddenly seemed to belong to the remote

BELOW *The jukebox, teenagers and the "American way of life" as portrayed by* Laugh *comic.*

ABOVE *Wurlitzer bought color and glamor to even the drabness of* On the Waterfront *(1954).*

past. When we look at the later 1940s Wurlitzers, we are truly seeing the "light of other days."

Although 1946 was dominated by Wurlitzer, the other companies were producing jukeboxes that were, for varying reasons, important. AMI, in particular, is remembered for its eccentric Model A, affectionately (?) known as the "Mother of Plastic." In jukebox design the only essential rules are dictated by practical considerations: the position of the title strips, selector buttons and coin entry (and, sometimes, the barely considered fact that the servicemen have to be able to repair the machine). Otherwise, designers are free to package the works in any way they want. To succeed, a jukebox has to be user-friendly and approachable. Yet at the same time it must have hidden reserves, the ability to look "alive," so that the novelty doesn't become stale and the patron's eyes are constantly drawn to the machine. The "perceived value" must be high: a big machine must justify its size, a small one project a presence that belies its lack of it. Aesthetics do not really enter the discussion: the "great" jukeboxes we have been looking at so far were of wildly differing shapes and sizes, and the public's only preconceived idea of what a jukebox should look like was that it should be "jukeboxy." (We saw how Wurlitzer's attempts to produce "olde-worlde" jukeboxes, with its 780 and 1080 models, failed. The public did not want "period charm" in a jukebox: they wanted entertainment.)

The AMI Model A seemed to try too hard. It was big in a blowzy sort of way. The upper plastics, deeply molded patterns in opaque white, represented an innovation, yet somehow they were reminiscent of globs of marshmallow. The speaker was at the top of the machine, so the speaker grille had to be above the mechanism, with the bottom half taken up by fluted plastic panels, divided by a narrow triangle of wood on which was mounted a decorative aluminum casting studded with theatrical "jewels." The lower panels were illuminated by turning colored cylinders, and the rest of the plastics by colored fluorescent

RIGHT *AMI's "Mother of Plastic," the classic of jukebox kitsch.*

lights. The buttons were set in flat aluminum panels, the surfaces of which, covered as they were in an elaborate pattern of scrolls and squiggles, only added to the impression that decoration had been thrown at the machine. The cabinet itself was no more than a thin walnut-finished shell, reinforcing one's feeling that the jukebox lacked depth, that it was little more than a façade of plastic behind which was a vast emptiness. The final impression is of some matron out on the town, with her tinted candy-flossed hair and costume jewelry aglitter. Nevertheless, the Model

ABOVE LEFT *"Barrel," "Trash Can" and "Washing Machine" are the common nicknames for the P146-148 Seeburgs.*

ABOVE RIGHT *First introduced to accompany the "Trash Can" series as the economy version of the roadhouse speaker, the "Teardrop" continued into the 1950s and became a feature of countless diners.*

"You don't want to watch things like this," said Cherie, "else you'll grow up mean, jest like all my brothers."

ABOVE *Marilyn Monroe, in* Bus Stop *(1956), appears to be warning against "Trash Cans."*

A sold well at the time, and many people are still very fond of it.

If the 1946 AMIs were extreme in one direction, that year's Seeburg was extreme in another. The Seeburg 146–148 series are striking examples of that purity of design which would be a feature of most of the company's jukeboxes from this time on. The

Model 146 was a logical successor to the pre-war "Hi Tones," developing the "in the round" look until the effect was almost cylindrical – hence the nickname of "The Barrel." As with the rest of the 1940s Seeburgs, the mechanism was not on view. Three years later it was to be very exposed, and it would remain so throughout the 1950s, but at the time it seemed a good idea to "knock" the success Wurlitzer had enjoyed with visible mechanisms. According to the publicity blurb,

> The time is past when the public is entertained by watching a selector mechanism. Musical taste and public discrimination have advanced, and as the novelty of coin-operated phonographs has worn off, there is more and more insistence on quality musical reproduction.

Seeburg was at the time developing its "universal music" system, and it is likely that the 20-selection 146–148 series of jukeboxes represented little more than a stopgap. Even so, the 146 was as uncompromising and solid as one would expect from Seeburg. The cabinet, finished in a dark, rich burl-walnut effect, continued the curve of the front through to the sides. Linkage was provided by side columns of

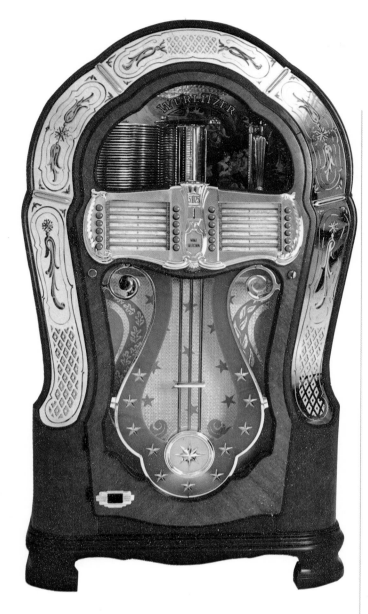

ABOVE *Although it avoided the austerity of the Model 780, Wurlitzer's second attempt at an "olde worlde" jukebox, the Model 1080, was nevertheless unsuccessful.*

Rising out of the top of the cabinet was the dome, a mushroom top of glowing red topped with a three-paneled chrome casting. The center panel read simply "Seeburg"; the two side ones were tapered teardrop lozenges. The entire dome top hinged open for loading the records – hence the series' nicknames of the "Washing Machine" and the "Trash Can." Centered beneath the dome were a simple coin-entry and construction plate, flanked by the titles. Here, Seeburg copied AMI's "Singing Towers," incorporating the titles in the buttons, which curved round to follow the contours of the cabinet's front. The front door incorporated an elegant and restrained casting set in a mosaic of small, square blue mirrors.

In 1946 Rock-Ola likewise launched the first of what was to be a series of three related models. This, the Model 1422, was perhaps the last American Art Deco-inspired jukebox. Returning to a more normal size after the massive "Commandos" and "Premiers" of 1942, the 1422 showed its changer mechanism, something which had been concealed in Rock-Olas since the late 1930s. The bright plated mechanism, set against an Art Deco-styled back screen, gave the jukebox a more open look. The ribbed outer plastics, molded in a translucent pale amber and illuminated at the sides with colored turning cylinders, likewise distanced the model's appearance from the rather heavy, bulbous look of the models Rock-Ola had produced earlier in the 1940s. In a further move toward the "lighter" style, the selector buttons were laid out in a simple row. Above the buttons, the title strips were lined up at an oblique angle, so minimizing the space they took up. However, the *pièce de résistance* of this model was the front grille. Rivaled only by that of the Wurlitzer 700, it was an outstanding example of the (by then rather dated) American Art Deco style. The central column was of fret-cut walnut, and in the top section revealed the colored plastic panel behind. On either side was the boldly styled metal grille, the bottom half open to show the speaker screen and the top backed with multicolored

back-lit bright-red plastic which contoured around toward the back; illuminated by a series of small bulbs rather than by fluorescents, they glowed like flames running up the machine, an effect emphasized by the small "flame" motifs in chrome that linked the main side plastics to the smaller, backward-sloping ones. The less respectful begged to differ: they said the side columns looked more like robot arms hanging down.

plastic, the panels of which changed hue as the color cylinders behind it revolved.

Wurlitzer greeted 1947 with, of course, a new model – the 1080. The 1015 was a hard act to follow, requiring something pretty radical. As we have seen, before the war Wurlitzer had established a marketing strategy which involved each new model rendering its predecessor outmoded – a stylistic planned obsolescence which was to become a feature of consumer items in the 1950s (particularly in the automobile industry). Yet, if the 1015 had betrayed its pre-war design, this was even more the case with the 1080, the last example of Paul Fuller's elaborate style. Named the "Colonial," it was – like the 780 before it – an attempt to produce a jukebox suited to the "conservative" locations. However, the lessons of the 780

ABOVE *Zenith's Cobra tone arm represented a landmark in sound reproduction. Initially for home phonographs, it was adopted by Wurlitzer for the Model 1100.*

had been learned, and the 1080 was no piece of pseudo-antique furniture but very much a jukebox.

Fuller's work typically betrayed a love of the Baroque, and (with the exception of the stately 780) aimed for the total theatrical effect. He had a flair for lighting and animation. His metalwork, although perfect in context, was heavily derivative of architectural metal of the 1930s, of the sort used on decorative elevator doors. His chief love was wood.

The 1080 had the most elaborate jukebox cabinet ever made, containing not a single vertical line in its extensive series of serpentine curves and bows. In total contrast with the 1015, no decorative metal broke up the flowing lines. The front grille was a graceful stylized lyre. Above the grille, the titles, buttons and coin entry were set in a sweeping embellished casting. Even the mechanism window followed the contours of the cabinet Behind the mechanism, the back mural was an "18th-century" Poussin-style picture. And, just in case the cabinet work was too subtle, the outer corners were set with mirrored plastic panels which resembled "opera-style" engraved glass (this latter effect, rather unfortunately, makes the whole machine seem a bit like a European gypsy caravan).

Despite the glow of the advertisements' "a period masterpiece rich in old world charm," the 1080 was a slow seller. Like its predecessor, the 780, it too was "held over." However, for the next year, 1948, it was updated to incorporate the latest technology.

BELOW *"Go in and join the fun."*

The Model 1080A, as it was designated, contained the same sound system as the 1948 Model 1100, featuring the revolutionary new Cobra tone arm. The Cobra, manufactured by the Zenith Corporation and already in use in that company's own domestic record player, was ideal for jukeboxes, which had hitherto used heavy tone arms (and needles which had to be frequently replaced). To record collectors, the sight of a 78rpm record that has been heavily "juked" is a sad one. Quite often, although one side is perfect, the other has been ground away, the shiny black shellac reduced to a dull gray. With the Cobra this was no longer a problem:

ABOVE *1948 was the last of the "Wurlitzer years" and the 1100 Paul Fuller's last jukebox design.*

The public plays the average popular numbers on your phonograph from 1,500 to 2,500 times. With conventional pick-ups the fidelity of those records starts to fall off at from 50 to 300 plays, and from that point, falls off FAST. You have to replace that record 3 or 4 times during the life of that tune. Not so with the Zenith Cobra Tone Arm! One record will play the entire run. That record will have 95 per cent fidelity after 2,000 plays. Will still be suitable for secondary spots or for resale.

ABOVE *The "Encore" program selector was a novel feature of the 1100.*

In adopting the Cobra, whose slender black curve tapers to a "snake's head" – including two little eyes – Wurlitzer was belatedly coming to terms with technology. Apart from introducing electric selection and making occasional modifications to the amplification systems, in the pre-war years Wurlitzer had been repackaging the same basic jukebox. The 1948 Model 1100 was a radically rethought machine, and, in tacit admission that the 1015 and 1080 were essentially pre-war designs, Wurlitzer announced "The World's first post-war phonograph is here!" Their advertisement showed the figure of the old year looking on as the baby 1948 made a selection on an 1100.

However, 1948 was to be the last year that would see Wurlitzer on top of the market for, however innovative the 1100 might be, it was to prove no match for the new jukebox concept Seeburg was preparing. With a sad appropriateness, it was also to be the last jukebox designed by Paul Fuller. It was fitting, too, that having first come to prominence way back in 1937 with the Model 24, the first light-up Wurlitzer, he should have as his swansong the last Wurlitzer to be dominated by moving light. In the 1100 this was achieved through a new approach to the cabinet, which became a thin shell elegantly rounding to a Gothic-arch top. The entire front door was a metal frame, painted to simulate wood. The top half of the door was taken up by a molded window, which was enormous – at least, by the standards of the time. For some reason, Wurlitzer's copywriters seemed to think that the public was still fascinated by wartime imagery (they were not: the jingoism had passed), and so they wrote of this window that the "panoramic sky top . . . built like a bomber's nose . . . gives everyone a ringside seat as the record changer mechanism works its magic in a dramatic, theatrical setting right before their very eyes." It is indicative of Wurlitzer's sense of security that it still believed the public would be fascinated with the familiar old mechanism, particularly as there was in fact something else that was worth watching – the new "Encore" program selector:

> A master stroke in multiplying play-appeal by making record selection faster, easier, more fun. Divides records into three programs of eight records each. Player makes selection from eight numbers showing on program holder. By pressing the master key, the program holder revolves and another selection of eight different numbers comes into view. New numbers appear above the selector buttons corresponding to the new set of eight tunes, and the color behind these numbers also changes to match the colored program numbers opposite the program slips. Action, motion, illumination combine in the Encore Program Selector, encouraging people to play the phonograph again and again.

This selector system, housed in a simple nickel molding, seemed suspended over the narrow, deeply angled speaker grille, which was flanked by faceted transparent plastics behind which were revolving color cylinders, emitting clean, bright light in prisms of ever-changing color.

Unfortunately, brilliant as the 1100 was, it came along just as a recession was hitting the jukebox industry. The post-war euphoria had not lasted long, and inflation had led to strikes. Some commentators argued that increased production was the best way to fight inflation, and the jukebox industry – especially

ABOVE *The P148 "Blondie" was the last of Seeburg's "Trash Can" series.*

Wurlitzer – had put such ideas into practice in a big way. Although this was justified in the immediate post-war period, operators having been starved of new machines since 1942, once things had settled down and the realities of the economy become apparent, it was plain that the future of the jukebox market was not going to be the non-stop bonanza many had expected.

Indeed, by early 1949 the jukebox industry was in a bad way. A contemporary article pinpointed the problem: "What is wrong with music? What will television, high prices, lower customer income, reduced amusement patronage, etc., do to music operations?" Summing up the post-war years, the writer comments:

ABOVE *The clean lines of the Wurlitzer 1100 caught the mood of the late 1940s.*

The industry was in a mad race to out-juke the juke, outsell the nearest competitor, undersell the nearest price level; out-entertain the most level entertainers. . . . Wartime pay and prosperity created a false sense of well-being which post-war market turbulence disturbed. . . . The drop from 24-hour wartime shifts with the pro-portionate decrease in pay; the mustering out of the military with its consequent loss of free spending; the readjustment of wartime travel and high life to previously normal ratios caught many good people in a spot where some lacked the judgment and good luck to guess right. [H. Carr, *The Coin Machine Journal*, January 1946.]

During this period, some of the smaller companies involved in jukebox production went under, and the others, including the Big Four, were content just to survive using variations on their immediate post-war models. Seeburg, for example, followed the 146 with the 147, which was basically the same save for a slightly restyled front grille and the replacement of the wooden front door with a metal one. For 1948's Model 148 they revamped it, making the entire cabinet out of metal. In early versions this was finished in dark walnut, like the 146 and 147, but almost all 148s were finished in a pale honey-colored wood effect, so earning the machine the nickname "Blondie." For the 148 the top dome too was revamped, the "mushroom" look being lost in a series of ripples, under which a color cylinder created beams of moving color.

Rock-Ola similarly updated its post-war range, with the 1426 and then the 1428. The 1426, which appeared in 1947, was basically the 1422 but with the wooden central grille replaced by a metal one featuring "Mother of Plastic"-style jewels. The Art Deco mural was done away with, to be replaced by a gaudy, diamond-quilted, gold-colored fabric embellished with "diamonds" (panels of colored mirror jewels). Only the side pilasters featured turning cylinders.

The 1426 was followed in 1948 by the 1428, which, while it kept the same cabinet form as the 1422 and 1426, had in fact been considerably revamped. Gone was the Art Deco grille (by now looking very dated), and in its place was a central vertical plastic molding, back-illuminated by a single color cylinder; on either side of the molding was an open lattice of diamond shapes revealing the patterned speaker screen. The chunky wooden front door of the 1422 and 1426 had been discarded in favor of metal painted in a grained pale-wood effect in the same manner as the Seeburg "Blondie." Like the AMI Model A, the 1428 indulged in deeply molded plastics. The top arches were of a rich turquoise color,

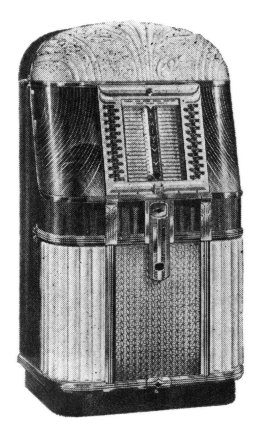

ABOVE *The AMI Model B had none of the blowzy brightness of the "Mother of Plastic."*

the lower pilasters of a fiery red, and the whole was framed in fancy but rather tinny chromework. As an example of the "flash" 1940s comic-strip style of jukebox which was to be so quickly outmoded, it was one of the best, and certainly it was the most colorful Rock-Ola ever.

AMI, in the meantime, was retreating from the garish bad taste of the Model A. In 1947 they brought out the B. Although the ribbed, illuminated bottom panels were retained, they were not so wide, and the grille they flanked was inoffensive. The rodeo jewelry was left off. The buttons and title strips were consolidated in a plain metal square which followed the line of the bottom plastics and was divided up the middle by a single fluorescent. This central section was flanked by two windows on which were screened fine bands of gold and through which the mechanism could be seen (these replaced the A's single central window). The whole jukebox was crowned by an ornate opalescent plastic molding whose deep molded patterns revealed its parentage.

ABOVE *As Wurlitzer had done, Rock-Ola featured the jukebox as a social focal point.*

Also in 1947, AMI brought out a new console for its "Automatic Hostess" system (Rock-Ola never reintroduced "Mystic Music"). However, as a means of offering a wider range of music, the telephone or wired method was soon to be rendered obsolete by something Seeburg had been developing since 1941, the "Industrial and Commercial Music System." By using an entirely new record-changer mechanism, Seeburg could now accommodate 50 records, both sides being playable. It introduced its new system in 1948 as a way of providing background music, but the implications for the jukebox industry were obviously staggering. Yet, incredible though it may now seem, the industry had become conditioned into thinking that all a jukebox really needed was a small choice of "pop music," and regarded the extra choice of records on offer merely as a means of catering to the off-peak trade:

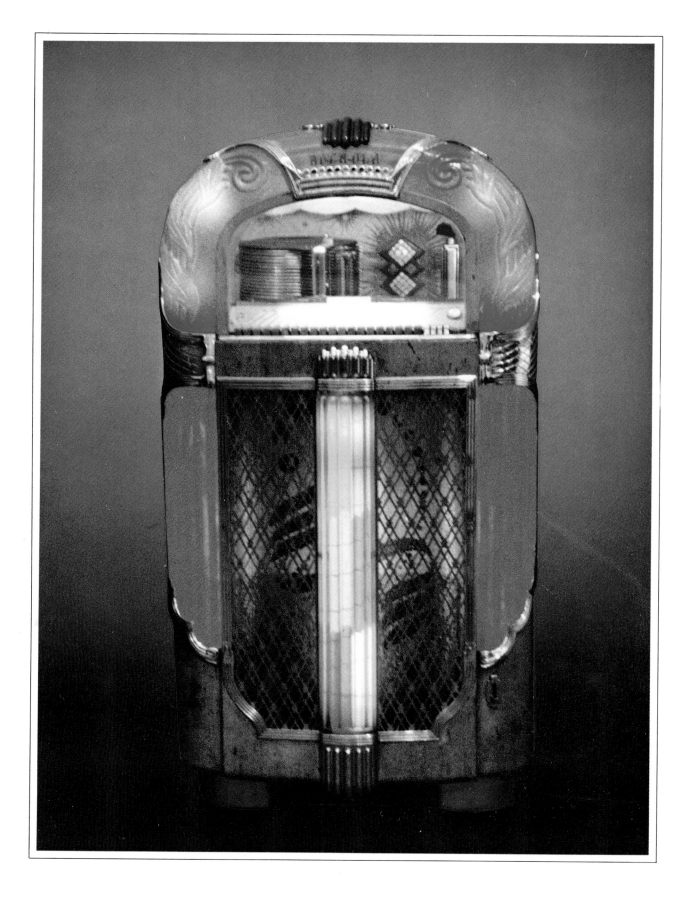

ABOVE *In Model 1608, the "Tone-o-lier" chandelier speaker accompanied the Rock-Ola Model 1428.*

A machine offering fifty records or a hundred selections would in no way decrease the average pop-record selections of the regular juke trade. Or as one might say the "after ten o'clock crowd". . . .

The "sustainer" type program is one of such a nature that it can be handled in numerous ways, yet provide revenue to the operator in non-peak periods as well as the peak periods, without additional cost or interference with the popular programs that are inherently jukebox items. Many locations, as all operators know all too well, in order to fill a gap in their music routine, had to install auxiliary systems. In some instances they subscribed to wired services of one kind or another. Others bought expensive electric or pipe-organ equipment which required a high-priced musician for short play periods . . . thus it is that a unit which would almost invariably carry the recordings of the so-called better or classical music would provide the means of supplying any type of location with background music, dinner music or special-occasion music in whatever choice of recordings one might desire. [Harvey Carr, *The Coin Machine Journal*, January 1946.]

LEFT *Ornately patterned plastic and a light cabinet marked a great leap forward by the Rock-Ola Model 1428 from the company's earlier post-war models.*

ABOVE *The new styling on the Model 1426 included a decorative metal grille.*

Still suffering from a social inferiority complex, the operator would instantly rise in status:

Such a system would automatically lift an operator out of the category of juke operator to entrepreneur of music. His library would be organized for quick service to the location of preselected programs for afternoon teas, birthday parties, anniversaries, children's parties, club meetings, even religious meetings. . . .

Despite the rosy picture presented to the future "entrepreneur of music," the coin-operated version of the "Industrial and Commercial Music System." the M100A, was very much a jukebox, albeit one that was to change history in much the same way that the introduction of sound had revolutionized the movies — spelling nemesis for some much-loved stars, but ultimately proving to be a savior.

5 INTO THE FUTURE

Seeburg's M100A represented the emergence of the "modern" jukebox. Although at the time it may have appeared that, after the incandescent beauties produced during the 1940s, by some strange reversal of nature the butterfly had changed into a larva, today we can more fully appreciate the uncompromising, sanitized lines of Nils Miller's new-look cabinet, immunized as we are by time from the cultural (and commercial) shock it initially caused. Here the jukebox, stripped to essentials, illustrates the puristic design adage that "form follows function."

Whereas the old sliding tray mechanism, sturdily built and severely practical, had been hidden from the public gaze, now, for the first time since the 1930s, Seeburg put its mechanism on full view. This new mechanism was spectacular in its apparent simplicity, particularly to a jaded audience which was beginning to regard progress as its birthright. By comparison, all the other changers suddenly showed their age, becoming mechanical antiques like some dusty automata from a fairground. In the M100A the records (all 50 of them) stood ready along the back of the machine, slotted into a bright red metal rack, their black rims shining out between the dividers. The playing mechanism, housed in a plastic molding that revealed only the tone arm and the turntable, traversed the cabinet to pick the records from the rack. On arriving at the appropriate spot, it would pull the record from the rack out onto the turntable, where it would spin edge-on to the viewer. The slender, vertical tone arm, equipped with two styli so that it could play either the "A" or "B" side, tracked in an apparently effortless defiance of gravity. After playing, the record was returned to its slot, and the machine was ready for the next selection.

Because the movement of the changer was lateral, the jukebox had to be wider than normal, but this was almost an advantage, a visual pun emphasizing that it carried a wide selection of music. Undoubtedly Seeburg, employing as it did so many expatriate

ABOVE *The "Select-o-matic" – "the greatest development in coin-operated phonographs."* **RIGHT** *Seeburg's revolutionary "Select-o-matic" mechanism was complemented by a new-look cabinet. This advertisement for the Model 100A dates from 1949.*

Swedes, would have been very aware of the new clean designs for domestic and office furniture emanating from Scandinavia at the time. The M100A showed the influence of these in its radical cabinet styling: slab-sided, topped with a shallow curved-glass window across its entire width, the cabinet was finished in a zebra-wood pattern, as with the "Blondie." This time, however, the stripes of the grain formed an integral part of the design: sometimes, as on the sides, they alleviated flat areas; elsewhere, particularly on the grille surround, they emphasized the razor-sharp angular planes.

The grille itself consisted of parallel narrow strips of bright metal bordered by a raked frame. Hidden above it, a multicolored screen diffused a fluorescent light in a rainbow of chevron-shaped reflections. A small motor made the diffuser rock backward and forward, so that a constantly moving pattern of colored light coursed up and down the grille. Although the concept was simple, it represents one of the most

Biggest news ever for Music Operators!

Seeburg MUSIC SYSTEMS "SELECT-O-MATIC 100"

YEARS AHEAD OF EVERYTHING IN COIN-OPERATED MUSIC!

THE MECHANISM IS IN FULL VIEW!

Year after year Seeburg has introduced new perfections in coin-operated phonographs..to gradually include all features operators have asked for. The new Seeburg "Select-O-Matic 100" is absolutely the last word, the most brilliant achievement in commercial music. The revolutionary "Select-O-Matic 100" has everything. Not 20 or 40 selections..but 100 selections..10-inch and 12-inch records may be mixed..selections may be catalogued in logical groups: (**1**) *hit tunes*, (**2**) *old favorites*, (**3**) *waltzes and polkas*, (**4**) *fox trots and rhumbas*, (**5**) *classical music*.

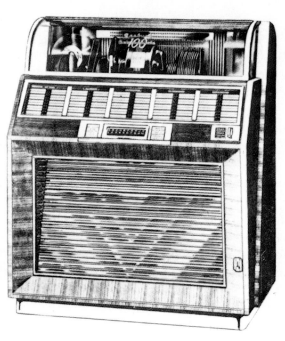

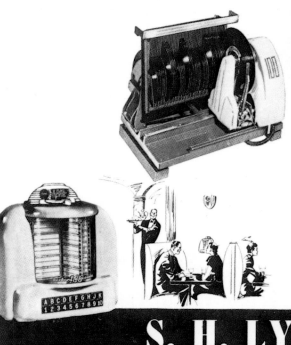

★ The public will thrill to watch the mechanical brain play 10-inch and 12-inch records vertically..either side or both sides with the same pick-up arm..in full view.

★ The "Wall-O-Matic 100" represents the most amazing remote selection system you have ever seen! 100 selections..visible 20 at a time. Single coin chute for nickels, dimes, quarters. 6 individual plays for a quarter. Push-button panel permits easy selection..uses only 20 push-buttons for 100 selections!

★ Strikingly beautiful appearance! The "Select-O-Matic 100" is brilliant in appearance with the top section providing full view of the Select-O-Matic mechanism. 100 selections visible at same time! Cabinet is luxurious wood veneer that skillfully blends with the animated grill that sends forth a constantly changing pattern of soft lights.

S. H. LYNCH & CO.
Exclusive Southwest Seeburg Distributors

★ **Dallas**, Pacific at Olive   ★ **San Antonio**, 241 Broadway   ★ **Oklahoma City**, 900 North Western
★ **Houston**, 910 Calhoun Street   ★ **New Orleans**, 832 Baronne Street   ★ **Memphis**, 1049 Union Avenue

successful uses of light in jukebox history, adding just the right color and movement without detracting from the machine as a whole.

Centered above the grille frame, the small, square, back-illuminated selection buttons were compactly grouped within a simple chrome frame. This in turn was flanked by the instruction windows, whose design was echoed in that of the coin slot, which was located at the extreme right. Sloping up toward the bottom edge of the mechanism window were the 50 double-title strips, spanning the width of the cabinet in serried rows. Rising up behind them was the mechanism that heralded the end of the 1940s jukebox and gave birth to the 1950s jukebox. For, although the M100A must have seemed to the other manufacturers like a death-knell, it was in fact to guarantee the future of the jukebox through what was to become one of its most exciting periods.

So close were the links and so logical the development from the M100A to the M100B that it is tempting to assume that the M100A was metamorphosed into the M100B as if by some simple evolution. However, if we are to appreciate the importance of the M100B we must now step back momentarily to look at it in its historical context.

Since the end of World War II, materials whose development had been accelerated for military use began to be used more and more for domestic consumer items. This was particularly true of the new plastics. In retrospect, the 1950s can be seen as the "plastic age." Plastics featured in home furnishings, domestic items and automobile interiors; paradoxically, jukeboxes made less use of plastics than they had during the 1940s. However, just as the innovation of translucent plastic in the late 1930s had made possible the "romantic age" of light-ups, so, a decade later, improved plastics technology was to give rise to a new era, the "silver age" of the 1950s. This time, though, the revolution concerned not the machines but the records. The shellac from which the old 78rpm discs were made was already causing prob-

ABOVE *As 45s replaced 78s, the jukebox remained the inspiration for countless songs.*

lems for the record manufacturers. It had been unavailable as a raw material during the war, and so old records had been scrapped and recycled. After the war it was once more readily available, but it was relatively expensive at a time when the market demanded cheap records.

The record industry was watching as the average age (and, by implication, spending power) of the record-buying public dropped, and — unable of course to anticipate rock'n'roll and the whole 1950s teen scene — came to the conclusion that the real future lay not with the single but with the LP. Leisure competition from television was already a factor that could only get worse as more and more people acquired the trappings of the "new" United States. Social patterns were changing, too, and the housing crisis of the time was being tackled through the building of the new suburbs. So, from a late-1940s viewpoint, one's prediction of the future could reasonably be that the majority of the new consumers would be spending their leisure time enjoying their newly built, newly furnished homes, equipped with all the latest labor-saving devices, and watching television. As for music, LPs of musical shows and light classics would be the industry's staple diet, while the single would cater solely to the lower-spending end of the market. As there was a general feeling that the jukebox might soon be a thing of the past, the major record companies felt that the matter of discs for the machines kids dropped nickels into was a pretty low priority. To cater to the more sophisticated home-leisure market was more important, and it was clear that it could not be done with discs in the old 78rpm format,

which allowed only a few minutes' playing time per side. Replacing shellac with vinyl enabled the record to be pressed with much closer grooves, and in 1948 Columbia introduced the 33⅓rpm LP.

The next stage in record development, although it was not generally recognized at the time, was to revolutionize the jukebox. In 1949 RCA introduced the seven-inch 45rpm disc. A trade report of the time makes amusing reading today:

At a special showing February 14th RCA Victor, Chicago area, held a special showing and press conference on the new 45rpm records. The initial offerings on these records are for the consumer trade, but it was intimated during the showing that something of interest to operators of phonographs would be coming in a reasonable time. A study of the new-type record would indicate that considerable improvements in records and record playing will be made in the future. As one manufacturer put it, the new smaller records have met a 50-year challenge. Amongst the advantages of the new records, other than fine tone quality, are extreme light weight, ease of handling with flexibility of selection programs. The new records have a large center hole which makes them easy to handle by young and old, by the clumsy as well as the skillful. One of the troubles with the old-style records was the difficulty in finding the spindle particularly if the machine was in operation.

These new records are made up in different color combinations so that symphony music, blues, race, country, ballads, etc., each has its own distinctive color. The records are also non-breakable. The weight factor alone is an important item, and when this type of record is adapted to the coin phonograph it will be a great improvement and permit operators to cut their service costs. [*The Coin Machine Journal*, February 1949.]

BELOW *Seeburg celebrated their 50th anniversary with the Model 100C.*

Exactly what changes to the record were envisaged to make it suitable for jukeboxes was not explained – after all, "adapted" to be compatible with the existing machines it would have to be a 10-inch 78! As it turned out, the problem never had to be solved. In October 1950 Seeburg introduced the M100B, the first 45rpm jukebox. The new age had dawned.

It is difficult today to imagine the risks Seeburg was taking when it committed itself to the 45rpm disc: even with the might of RCA behind the new-style record, its success was not guaranteed. The industrial climate was uncertain. Once more the country was at war, this time in Korea, and against a background made up of the draft, the return to war production and the national fear of an escalation into global conflict, jukeboxes seemed all set to return to their World War II role as a beacon of cheer in times of despair. In troubled times the great advantage of a jukebox over television, radio or cinema is that you don't hear any bad news! However, to curtail production of jukeboxes in favor of war work would lose Seeburg all the impetus it had gained through developing the M100A. Seeburg's dilemma was a major one. In the event, jukebox production was not interrupted. Indeed, when it came to choosing from the new 1950 models the operator was presented with an even greater confusion of style and technology than ever before.

All eyes were on the M100B, which was in every way a new box. Although superficially it seemed a scaled-down M100A, subtle styling changes insured that this was a new model in terms of many things other than the records it was designed to play. As though to emphasize the lightness and smaller size of the 45rpm discs, the cabinet was narrower and brighter. The rainbow grille, carried over from the M100A, was now framed by a mosaic of rectangular

*The links between the Wurlitzer Model 1250 (**ABOVE**) and the Seeburg Model 100A (**RIGHT**) are obvious in the two machines' cabinet styling, as we can see in this pair of contemporary photographs.*

mirrors inlaid into the surround. The reduced width meant that, in order to accommodate the title strips, two frames of five double-title lines had to be dropped down to either side of the button bank, adding to the overall effect of compactness. To drive the message home, decals on the lid glass proclaimed: "The World's First Commercial Mechanism Designed Exclusively to Play 45rpm Records." Such was the novelty that it was felt necessary also to show a picture of the new 45rpm record!

At the same time as the M100B's launch, Seeburg announced that M100A machines could be returned to be converted to 45rpm.

As the Seeburg company triumphantly entered the 1950s, the other manufacturers were watching their customers desert them in favor of the M100B. Customer loyalty in the jukebox business was a tradition, but it was a tradition based on dollars rather than sentiment. The relationship between a distributor and an operator might have as its basis advantageous finance and trade-in terms; the maintenance engineers would be familiar with a particular mechanism and know the manufacturer's way of doing things, while a collection of appropriate spare parts would have built up. Wurlitzer, in particular, had done much to exploit the glory-by-association concept, whereby it was implied that operating jukeboxes which were so much in the public eye enhanced the status of the operator, yet now it seemed that there was little glory left in Wurlitzer. The 1100 and 1080A models had not been commercial successes, the Wurlitzer management had changed, and Paul Fuller was retiring in bad health. Joseph Clements, who was to be Wurlitzer's chief stylist throughout the 1950s, had replaced Fuller as head of design; the 1250, his 1950 model, was his first project in that capacity.

In terms of style, Wurlitzer was not yet ready to abandon its "romantic" look, and in many ways the 1250 was a retrogressive step, rejecting the clean profile of the 1100 and reintroducing decorative concepts that essentially belonged to the pre-war period.

The cabinet echoed – or, rather, parodied – that of the Seeburg M100A, taking as its starting point the full-width mechanism window, which curved down and then inward, so that it looked almost like a cylinder of clear plastic (seen from the side, even more so) incorporated with the curves of the cabinet.

However, whereas in Seeburg's M100A the wide cover housed a mechanism that traversed the machine, under the 1250's imposing canopy was the familiar old Simplex mechanism. A second tone arm had been added to play the "B" sides of the records, so that the effective selection capacity was doubled to 48. In fact, the proportions of the cabinet invite speculation that Wurlitzer may have contemplated increasing the height of the record stack: there is enough space for a further 12 selections.

As a stopgap measure the 1250 was ingenious enough – Rock-Ola followed much the same course – but the styling as a whole made the mechanism seem even more ungainly than it actually was. Beneath the rather bulbous top were the buttons and titles, set in chunky nickel castings. The grille was of the open-lattice type, similar to that on the Rock-Ola 1428, revealing behind it a finely perforated speaker screen printed so as to simulate tapestry. Obviously Wurlitzer was reluctant to abandon the decorative element that had been so much the signature of Paul Fuller, because it had a pair of illuminated and colorfully patterned plastic screens extending the grille area to either side, and these were in turn flanked by massive nickel-plated fluted columns.

As a piece of pure design the Model 1250 is appalling: seen next to the M100A or even Wurlitzer's own Model 1100 it is an ungainly compromise. In its own way, however, it was rather magnificent, and the pilasters, borrowed in simplified form from the Seeburg 100C, 100G and 100W models, and later referred to in several subsequent Wurlitzers, became a key design feature of 1950s jukeboxes.

The advent of the 100A and 100B was probably less traumatic for Rock-Ola and AMI, whose position

in the market had never been hyped in the same way as Wurlitzer's had been.

Rock-Ola's 1950 model, the 1432 "Rocket," represented a radical shift from previous designs, a more profound acknowledgment of the new age than Wurlitzer had been prepared to make. The mechanism was basically the same as before (the advertisements sought to make this a virtue, describing it as "time-tested"), but the addition of another five trays and a second tone arm upped the number of selections to 50. Although the "Rocket" was still basically a 78rpm player, conversion to 33⅓rpm or 45rpm records was offered. The cabinet echoed the Seeburg M100A in its full-length sloping sides and in its recognition that the new "Scandinavian" look was about lightness and simplicity; the blond finish of the 1428 was retained, but the fancy plastics and decorative metalwork were discarded. Even the name – "Rocket" – was very much of the period (Oldsmobile used it for its famous 1951 Rocket 88), associating the jukebox with the popular optimism that the 1950s were going to be bright and innovative, the precursors of the Space Age.

The 1951 Seeburg, the M100BL, was essentially the M100B with cosmetic changes. A paler wood finish, lacking the zebra stripes, was used on the cabinet (The "L" stood for light). The mechanism was finished in a rich emerald green. This machine was in production for less than a year.

In 1952 Seeburg seemed to have decided that the austere look had gone far enough – besides which, it was their birthday! Exactly 50 years had passed since the foundation of the original J.P. Seeburg Co. and, although it had developed into a major company whose design and manufacturing capacity encompassed not only jukeboxes but amusement games,

vending machines and military hardware, it was still very much a family firm: Justus Seeburg himself, then 81 years old, was still active in the company. The occasion could not pass without a celebration. It was not in Seeburg's nature to go over the top and so, without the publicity with which Wurlitzer was later to surround its half-centenary, the company introduced the M100C as its anniversary model.

Although the M100C was not actually a birthday cake it was very pretty – one of the prettiest and yet most understated jukeboxes of all time. The top half – the curved window, title strips and button bank – was the same as in the M100B series, but the cabinet had been restyled, with the hard angles being dropped in favor of long sloping sides like those of the M100A. The bottom half, on the other hand, was conceptually new. The angled picture frame and horizontal grille strips had disappeared: in their place were pilasters (essentially a Wurlitzer hallmark) in translucent plastic illuminated by chain-driven colored turning cylinders. Although the turning cylinder had been a feature of jukebox design since the early 1940s, in this little 1950s masterpiece it looked as fresh as new. Between the pilasters lay the speaker grille, whose vertical silvery rods reflected the patterns of colored light. Although these machines are now often found with chrome-plated metal replacements, the rods were originally glass tubes which had been internally silvered.

The fragility of these original rods serves as a reminder to us that, despite the rough usage to which many jukeboxes were later subjected, they were initially conceived with solely the "good" location in mind. Throughout the history of the jukebox, manufacturers' brochures have invariably shown them in elegant surroundings, admired by well-dressed people. It was only later, with its KD model, that Seeburg would dare to have teenagers shown in promotional material. By then, though, the 1950s jukebox had become synonymous with rock'n'roll and the teenage rebel.

LEFT *Linking their advertising to the theme of prospecting, Wurlitzer described their Model 1250 as a "golden opportunity" for profits. Meanwhile, Seeburg had already staked their claim for the 1950s with the Model 100A.*

6 GEE, DAD, IT'S A WURLITZER

The year 1952 was important for Rock-Ola: the "Rocket" went into its second generation with the 1952 Model 1434 "Super Rocket." Although its styling was almost a complete copy of that of the Wurlitzer 1400, it was much more compact, and the concentration of the same elements – the faceted light-up pilasters and the open-look canopy – gave it a dynamic quality which the Wurlitzer lacked. Like the 1432, the 1434 was available as a 45rpm player.

The 1952 "Fireball" (Model 1436) was the first jukebox launched by Rock-Ola specifically as a 45rpm player. Rock-Ola's 120-selection changer mechanism was a perfect counter to the Seeburg Selectomatic, since it solved one of the major problems inherent in storing a large quantity of discs within a small space; the technique was subsequently adopted and adapted by AMI and Wurlitzer, enabling them to produce large-selection machines. The discs were slotted into a revolving vertical drum. Each divider had a spring-loaded catch which stopped the record dropping out but which flicked open when the record was in the play position at the top. As with the AMI machines of the time, a gripper arm then picked the record out, turning it one way or the other for the "A" or "B" side, and placed it on the turntable.

The novelty of the mechanism (not to mention the use of 45rpm records) would, Rock-Ola thought, rekindle the public's traditional fascination for seeing the jukebox do its stuff: "With this facility on your machines people will deposit coins again and again for the added attraction of watching it operate!" And, of course, as a neat bit of one-upmanship, Rock-Ola capped Seeburg's much-vaunted ability to provide 100 selections by offering 120 choices. To accommodate the title strips, Rock-Ola adopted the type of revolving display that Wurlitzer had used on the Model 1100.

The advent of the new Rock-Ola, although it was not as dramatic as that of Seeburg's M100A and M100B, was a major contribution to the establishment of the image of the 1950s jukebox. The industry's need was for a range of machines, meeting a variety of demands – from the "googie architecture" of the new coffee shops, whose patrons were enjoying the style-awareness of the early 1950s in their cars, clothes and home furnishing, to the small traditional bar serving perhaps a local farming community; likewise, the clients varied from the big operator with a professional sales team to site the latest jukebox in the best location down to the little man who delivered his machines from the back of a pick-up. Without an equal contribution of new models from the manufacturing giants and the consequently thriving second-hand market, the industry would not have survived.

Although Rock-Ola had taken the plunge by incorporating the new mechanism, the "Fireball" nevertheless drew its style from the late 1940s. Even the publicity material recalled that for the old Wurlitzer Model 1100, when it referred to the mechanism dome: ". . . as sleek and modern as the canopy of a jet plane, this Rock-Ola innovation gives customers a control tower view of the Fireball 120 revolving changer in action. . . ."

BELOW *Rock-Ola's Model 1436 was advertised as "the only phonogrph with 120 selections."*

ABOVE *David Rockola endorses the Model 1436.*

A change of cabinet was needed – and fast. The inspiration came from the Seeburg 100C. The 1953 Model 1438 "Comet-Fireball" is, unfortunately, nothing more than a parody of that classic. The cabinet is a close copy, and it likewise has illuminated pilasters. Even the grille rods – or, rather, the suggestion of them, for they are simulated in the half-round ribbing of the perforated metal grille – are naked imitations.

Meanwhile, the Seeburg company itself, never losing its momentum, had brought out a restyled version of the 100C. There were two models, 1953's 100W and HF100G. In these the curved glass of the lid was deeper, dropping down to cover the title strips,

which were in an angled rack back-lit by a single fluorescent lamp which also served to illuminate the mechanism. Along the front of the machine were selector buttons; rather than being small cubes, these were now piano-type keys. Of the two 1953 models, the 100W was the economy one, although that did not prevent it from having a great visual quality: ". . . flanking the chromium diamond studded grille are pilasters of modern fiberglass that spread a pleasing pattern of cool, refreshing illumination and color." These pilasters echoed the fiberglass "modern art" domestic light fittings which were at the time the latest look in home decor: although the jukebox industry had always been quick to assimilate new materials, it was unusual for something as ephemeral as decor lighting to have an influence.

If the fiberglass pilasters were symbolic of Seeburg's determination to produce truly modern jukeboxes, the Model HF100G proved the point. Although it was more conservatively styled than the slightly cheaper M100W, with chromium pilasters on either side of a pierced blue-painted grille instead of the light-up fiberglass, it featured a magic quality already being used in domestic sound equipment and all the rage at the time – High Fidelity. In an age when everything had to be newer, brighter and better than ever before, the consumers were eager for anything that was progressive: a simple styling change or a technological development was a sufficient excuse to junk the old and buy the new. Magazines, not to mention suburban parties, were full of instant ex-

ABOVE *The influence of the Seeburg 100C on the Rock-Ola "Comet-fireball" is obvious.*

perts talking of "woofers" and "tweeters," and the jukebox needed to demonstrate that the patron's nickel would give him or her the same quality of sound reproduction that the well-off were now enjoying at home. Of course, as this was the 1950s, the sound had to be not just "hi-fi," but "Deluxe hi-fi"!

Seeburg, which was normally quite reserved in its publicity, spoke of the HF100G in much the same way as if it were advertising a domestic hi-fi:

See . . . but more important . . . hear the new Selectomatic 100 Deluxe High Fidelity at your first opportunity. . . . You won't believe you're hearing the same records. . . . You'll think you're right in the studio with the recording artist. There's a new realism and presence . . . a faithfulness of reproduction . . . a third dimension . . . from the lowest lows to the highest highs . . . that will capture and hold the attention of even the most critical listeners. Matching this tonal perfection is the stunning appearance of the Deluxe High Fidelity, completely styled in the "new look" with smart distinctive chromium pilasters . . . another Seeburg first!

BELOW *Seeburg's HF100 was the first High Fidelity (hi-fi) jukebox.*

ABOVE *Modernistic fiberglass pilasters were the unique styling feature of the Seeburg 100W.*

While Seeburg was forging ahead, Wurlitzer was trying to recover the position it had had during the 1940s. Following the Model 1250, Wurlitzer returned to the cleaner lines it had established with the Model 1100. The 1951 models 1400 and 1450, although featuring a fancy grille and canopy valance, were spartan in comparison with the 1250. In both machines the cabinet had straight sides curving in toward the top. On the model 1400 it was in walnut and on the 1450 it was in "Texileather." "One of the modern materials in the fine furniture field," said the publicity material, "Texileather is scuff proof, water proof and alcohol proof. Available in standard mahogany or in blond, blue and brown colors to complement location interiors. . . ." This was the first time a cabinet had been offered in a range of colors. The front was simply the grille flanked by two faceted pilasters in the same manner as in the Model 1100. The transparent "drum-style" mechanism window of the 1250 was modified so that both ends were capped with curved sides, giving an in-the-round view of the mechanism. Unfortunately, the mechanism itself was the same as that used on the 1250, and so the public's enthusiasm for being able to see a bit more of the same old thing must have been distinctly

muted. Wurlitzer's publicists tried to brazen it out. For a start (they claimed), the Seeburg system was bad for record handling, whereas

. . . with the Wurlitzer every record rests flat on a tray — fully supported. No danger that the new, thin plastic records will chip, break or warp in a Wurlitzer as they do when stacked unsupported on their rims and picked up by their edges.

ABOVE *"You'll hear music you never knew was on the records."*

As for those 100 selections, who needed them?

Wurlitzer asked the operators — they told that 75 per cent of their income comes from eight or ten selections on a phonograph. Their answers were unanimous — "forty-eight tunes on twenty-four records is enough!" — additional records get little play, slow up selection, increase service costs.

Model 1450

ABOVE *The diamond-patterned pilasters and molded canopy of the Wurlitzer Model 1400 were reminiscent of the Model 1100.*

This statement carried echoes of Homer Capehart's comment when machines with 24 selections were first introduced: "That's all the music we'll ever need on a jukebox." Wurlitzer's bravado about the virtues of a small selection was short-lived, however, for in the very next year, 1952, it produced the Model 1500, which offered 104 selections! In more ways than one there was a change of tune:

> That it will prove the most profitable on location is obvious for it is literally alive with money-making features. First off it tops them all in number of records – plays one hundred and four selections – the greatest array of tunes to tempt all musical tastes in the history of this business. . . .

Although Wurlitzer had finally burst through the mega-selection barrier, the way in which it did so seems to have been born from desperation, and has little in common with the clean design solutions of

LEFT *Wurlitzer's 1450 version was available with cabinets finished in mahogany, blond, blue or brown "Texileather."*

Seeburg and Rock-Ola. What Wurlitzer did was, quite simply, to make the Model 1500 (or Model 1550 if in Texileather) a double jukebox. The twin tone arms were placed in the center of the changer, and on either side were the traditional Wurlitzer record stacks, to each of which had been added an extra two trays. The complications of this mechanical nightmare were compounded by the fact that the machine had the ability to mix record speeds: either a 78rpm or a 45rpm record could be played, the machine adjusting to the correct speed by means of the much-puffed "WURLIMAGIC BRAIN." Alternatively, the 1500 could be converted to play exclusively 33⅓rpm records, offering up to 26 hours of continuous play without any repetition.

The cabinet of the 1500 was necessarily considerably wider than that of the 1400, to accommodate the massive double changer. Instead of adopting Seeburg's logical approach – double title strips ("A" and "B" sides of each record listed on the same card) – Wurlitzer opted for single title strips. The result was an impressive display, but the great bank of titles spanning the front did nothing to alleviate the visual effect of the machine's enormous width. Below the titles was a bright, textured and perforated metal

BELOW *Operators were supplied with card holders featuring the "WURLIMAGIC BRAIN."*

speaker screen shimmering behind a grille of simple bars linked by wavy lines, with a large letter "W" in flowing script in the middle. On each side of this was a narrow glass pilaster decorated with stylized musical motifs.

Apart from anything else, the sheer size of this jukebox limited its appeal, and so in the same year Wurlitzer also offered restyled versions of 1951's 1400/1450 range, introducing a garish back mural in "day-glo" colors and a front grille of simple bars. It was very obvious that Wurlitzer was by now out of its depth in the new jukebox technology; perhaps even sadder, it had lost the quality of "absolute image" that had been so much a hallmark of the Wurlitzer style throughout the Paul Fuller years.

The 1500/1550 was brought out again the next year. Designated 1500A and 1550A, these 1953 Wurlitzer models featured a restyled top canopy: this was now a simple curved window, in exactly the same size as in the Seeburg M100A, M100B and M100C series. And, yes, Wurlitzer was still pushing the idea of the "fascinating" mechanism!

BELOW *The twin-stack system was a desperate bid by Wurlitzer to increase the capacity of the Simplex mechanism.*

The focal point of interest on any phonograph is the record changer compartment. That's where the wheels go "round" and that's what the public loves to see. On the Model 1500A they'll really see it through a super-size one-piece polished glass Astra Dome that puts all the color and action in this compartment on perpetual parade.

ABOVE *The Model 1550A, with the twin-stack system, was soon to be made obsolete by Wurlitzer's carousel mechanism.*

To replace the 1400 range in 1953 came the models 1600 and 1650, styled in a similar way to that year's 1500 range; the 1600 was an "all-speed machine" (although not intermixed), while the 1650 was available only for 45rpm. Carried over with minor cosmetic changes into 1954 as the 1600A and 1650A, these became available with a "High Fidelity" sound system (models 1600AF and 1650AF).

The machines in this rather uninspiring range were the last to house the old Simplex mechanism. By now an antique, Wurlitzer's old workhorse had served until it could carry on no longer. Now, at last, a new mechanism was ready to replace it. Like Rock-Ola's, the new Wurlitzer changer was a carousel, but it differed in that it lay flat instead of being upright. The mechanism was more complex and untidy than Rock-Ola's, but most of it was hidden beneath the carousel surround, and the bits that were on public view appeared to have an elegant simplicity. A semi-circular arch spanning the carousel carried the tone arm. Rising up from the center of the carousel was a fan-shaped metal casting, behind which was mounted the turntable. When a selection was made the carousel revolved, stopping at the appropriate place, whereupon one of two arms set on either side of the carousel would appear (depending upon whether an "A" or a "B" side was to be played) and push the record up into the vertical play position. The turntable began to spin and the tone arm moved over onto the record, which played in the vertical position, the tone arm tracking along it in apparent defiance of gravity.

Predictably — although at last with some justification! — Wurlitzer advertised the visual impact of the record changer: "People will pay just to watch its fascinating operation." The cabinet was basically very much the same as in the 1600 series but with a deep V-shaped grille screen that gave the bottom half a three-dimensional look. Still, the lack of innovation in the presentation hardly mattered: the important thing was the new mechanism, which at last freed Wurlitzer to develop a truly 1950s jukebox. From here on Wurlitzer would once again be in the forefront of jukebox design. The slogan used to launch this new machine was "Gee, Dad, it's a Wurlitzer." Soon this was a popular catchphrase. Wurlitzer was back!

TOP AND ABOVE *The machines in Wurlitzer's 1600 range were the last to use the Simplex mechanism.*

ABOVE. *Housed in a similar cabinet to that of the 1600 models, the Model 1700, with its new carousel changer, was widely advertised using the slogan "Gee, Dad, it's a Wurlitzer".*

ABOVE *The slogan even appeared as a button.*

appeared to hover. The mechanism itself was the standard Selectomatic, but its cover and the record housing were restyled for this model. In place of the old "jelly mold" mechanism cover, which had first appeared with the M100A and then, in scaled-down form, served the M100B through to the HFG, there was a square box-like structure. Instead of the back-lit "100-Selectomatic" window of the "jelly mold," the flat front of this cover consisted of small embossed squares of iridescent blue set in a "chrome" frame. A stylized Seeburg logo in red and a red "100" sur-mounted by "Selectomatic" in chrome were in relief against the background, catching the light shining up from the fluorescent light that also back-lit the title cards, adding life and sparkle to the mechanism.

It was not a moment too soon. In 1954 it was estimated that Seeburg's dominance of the market was such that 70 per cent of all new jukebox sales were of Seeburgs. And, in yet another dramatic design coup, Seeburg once more gave the jukebox a new style with the Model HF100R, the "Bandshell." Here, the back of the cabinet curved steeply forward to the top of the lid-glass frame, which in turn curved down to just above the button bank. The side glasses were framed in a large boomerang-shaped casting. The framework of the lid was narrow, and did not detract from the visual impact of the back of the machine curving over the mechanism — much like the cantilever roofs which were then becoming a feature used by the more adventurous architects. The interior of this curving back was lined in ribbed gold-anodized aluminum, and within it the mechanism

BELOW *"Gee, Dad, it's a Wurlitzer" became such a popular catch-phrase that even* Mad *magazine paid tribute to it in a parodied form.*

ABOVE *With the HF100R, Seeburg once again injected new style into the jukebox.*

The record magazine, too, was restyled: it was finished in a contrasting dark blue and the end caps were molded into truncated bullets of the sort beginning to appear in automobile design; as a final touch, circular windows of milky white bore "100" in blue letters. These windows lit up, so that the entire mechanism was highlighted in color.

Extra sparkle came from the treatment of the front grille. The speaker screen itself sloped back so that the button bank above it appeared to be jutting out. The screen was divided by three pairs of elaborate (by Seeburg standards) castings, ripples of chrome that shimmered under the fluorescent down-light. These were fronted by wedge-shaped panels of ribbed and textured glass – which also featured at either end of the grille.

Seeburg described the "Bandshell" as "the most beautiful, the most complete and the finest performing music system ever offered to the coin-operated music industry." The high-quality music reproduction

was a result of the machine's multispeaker system: as well as three speakers at the front the HF100R had two more mounted one on each side of the cabinet.

The basic form of the HF100R was perpetuated in the 1955 Model 100J which, later redesignated to acknowledge a light-color finish (100JL), continued to be produced until 1957; it was one of the most enduring cabinet styles of the 1950s. The major difference between the HF100R and the 100J was the

BELOW *This 1954 AMI advertisement reminded the trade that the company was the pioneer of double-sided play.*

front grille. Although the grille of the HF100R was beautiful, its glass screens were all too likely to get broken, so in the 100J the glass and decorative chrome castings were replaced by a simple rectangular grille of large diamond mesh set in a frame and mounted on vertical poles. This rather "utility" effect was an anticlimax after the splendors of the HF100R.

85

ABOVE *A diner featuring AMI remote selectors (about 1954).*

but in historical terms this hardly matters: both models were rapidly upstaged by the other 1955 Seeburg – the V200, which will be discussed at length in the next chapter.

Apparently undisturbed by the changes going on around them, AMI had continued to make sound, if undistinguished, jukeboxes. In terms of technology, AMI had the advantage in that its 1930s changer mechanism (modified at the time of the Model A) could handle 45rpm discs just as well as it did 78s.

Not only had AMI avoided expensive development costs, which would have necessitated volume sales at a relatively high unit price, but, unlike the others of the Big Four, it was not dependent on a distribution set-up. Even the smallest operators could buy their AMIs direct. AMI's relatively simple and reliable mechanism was the company's main selling point, one that made its machines particularly popular in the export markets. As late as 1956 AMI was still extolling the virtues of the A mechanism:

ABOVE *After the extravagance of the Model A AMI continued the toning down in style seen in the Model B with the more conventional C and D models.*

Here was a record changer that doubled the program at no extra cost for records. Acclaimed immediately by operators, it won instant and lasting regard. The rugged durability, functional simplicity and reliable performance of the AMI changer endured. Not only has this basic music mechanism been used in AMI jukeboxes since, but most of the original Model A jukeboxes are still operating profitably after 10 years – and at little or no costs for parts and service. Many operators got their start in the music business 10 years ago with the Model A – and have these self-same machines still on their routes. They are confident that 10 years of service has not – by far – exhausted the margins of quality built into every AMI record changer.

Strong though the engineering may have been, the styling of the AMI machines was totally devoid of glamour, and nor were any contemporary influences much in evidence.

The Model B, discussed earlier, had mutated into the C. The main changes were that the lower pilasters lost their ribbing, the grille was replaced by a louvered one, the cabinet top was rounded (Model 1015 style), and the white-top plastic of the B was replaced by a clear dome. Mirrors were used to allow the mechanism to be seen playing through the top window.

When lit, the Model C was an effectively pretty box, much as the B had been, but it allowed little room for development, and in 1951 it was superseded by the Model D. This had a rather bizarre cabinet, with the selector buttons and titles at the top and beneath them a steeply curved mechanism window, screened with a line of broad arrows pointing down to the coin entry immediately below. To make a selection the patron had to reach over this window. The arrows on the mechanism window gave the jukebox a vending-machine look. At the bottom, the machine was almost entirely taken up with chunky white plastic louvers that continued round to the sides of the cabinet: illuminated in changing colors, these successfully updated a theme unique to AMI since the times of the Model A – color diffused through opaque textured plastic.

BELOW *The simple lines of the E models represented a breakthrough for AMI's styling.*

the MODEL E·120

Height: 62½"
Width: 39⅝"
Depth: 26½"
Weight: 318 lbs.
Shipping Weight: 415

ABOVE *Typical AMI advertisements of 1954.*

However, with its finely finished walnut cabinet and bright aluminum metalwork, the E is close to the spirit of the Seeburgs of the early 1950s – a style which Seeburg itself had been progressively moving away from.

Although it was now nearing the midpoint of the decade, the 1950s jukebox still lacked the essential charisma which had established the machine's prominence during the 1940s. Its environment had changed and, whereas in the 1940s the constant flow of new models with their ever-changing designs and colors was exciting, because the rate of style change in other areas of daily life was relatively slow-moving, in the accelerated pace of the 1950s the jukebox was perceived by many people as nothing more than a familiar – and minor – entertainment device. By now those little chrome wallboxes, descendants of the

For 1953 the Model D was successfully modified into the Model E. The bottom half of the cabinet was retained, but the ostentatious curve of the mechanism window was reduced to make a subtle bow, the lines of which carried on to the top of the cabinet, so that the total effect was of the front of the jukebox gently sweeping back. Above the mechanism window was a neat row of selector buttons and title strips. The E was available with a choice of number of selections – 40, 80 or 120. The central width of the 120-selection model ruined the otherwise pleasing lines of this cabinet style.

The E range was a satisfactory conclusion to the quest for style which AMI had been pursuing since the A, and they had high hopes for it:

Ever since the repeal of prohibition many swank bars and elite restaurants have steadfastly refused to accept a jukebox of any kind. It took Model E by AMI to turn the tide. The deluxers have suddenly fallen for the E's breathtaking beauty, smart style and tonal fidelity and are telling AMI ops to "put one in."

BELOW *From* The Blackboard Jungle *(1955) to the "jukebox jungle" was but a short step.*

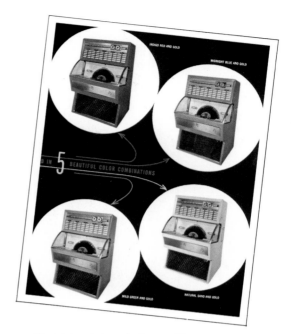

systems Seeburg and Rock-Ola had popularized, were commonplace, and increasingly they were not just an accessory of the jukebox but, used with a hideaway, were taking its place. The Wurlitzer image of happy throngs gathered around a jukebox was now an out-dated 1940s image.

There was, however, one group for whom the jukebox was a focal point: the devotees of the types of music that commercial censorship, to a large extent, banned from the radio. You would not be able to hear the blues, R&B and nascent rock'n'roll on the radio, but if you were lucky there might be some on your local jukebox. Throughout its history, the jukebox had played records that would not otherwise have had a public airing. Not on prime sites, of course, but by the time a jukebox had been downgraded a few times the operator was happy to stack it with whatever selections the patrons would pay to hear. The small independent record companies would look to the jukebox to give their discs exposure, and the nickels would drop in to play the "local hit." Sometimes these regional hits were quite parochial, even to the extent of incorporating advertising – a bar

ABOVE *The jukebox designed by Raymond Loewy, the "United."*

referred to by name, or a local beer by brand.

The youth cult which had first become apparent during the war years was by now a recognized social factor. Under the "youth" umbrella, the spoiled kids of suburbia shared with the poor and deprived a form of music they could call their own. The adoption of this "new" music by the young soon created an organized backlash. The events described in a 1955 press report – headlined "Obscene R&B Tunes Blasted" – are not atypical:

BELOW *The jukebox became a central image of the newly emergent rock 'n' roll.*

Connecticut police in Bridgeport and New Haven this week barred "rock and roll" dances and said they would issue no more permits for such affairs. Bridgeport's Superintendent of Police John A. Lyddy said the action was prompted by complaints from parents, adding, "Teenagers virtually work themselves into a frenzy to the beat of fast swing music." Meanwhile the Boston deejay censorship committee under the chairmanship of WVDA deejay Sherm Feller drew up a five-point statement after conferring with jazz expert Father O'Connor of Boston University's WBUR and Monsignor Lally. The boys avowed their awareness to keep disc programming clean for home consumption, and promised to keep a sharp alert for offensive lyrics. At the same time, though, they pointed out that jukeboxes and counter sales are making records available that have never been played on the air. Meanwhile, jukebox operators in Somerville, Mass., were also targets of civil displeasure. Under the supervision of the local police department headed by Lieut. Thomas O'Brien, a Crime Prevention Committee this week handed operators a list of tunes the law wouldn't allow them to carry on their machines. [June Bundy, *Billboard*, April 1955.]

Notices that had hitherto been used on gambling machines – "Minors are forbidden by law to operate this machine" – started appearing on jukeboxes. Radio stations, with their reliance on advertising revenue and their vulnerability to local pressure groups, increasingly dropped R&B and rock'n'roll from their playlists, leaving jukeboxes – which, outside a few areas such as hapless Somerville, were left largely uncensored – as the sole public source of the "new" music.

LEFT *Seeburg's magnificent V200, the last jukebox to be produced under the control of the Seeburg family.*

The public's worst fears, engendered by countless sermons and press articles, were realized when Evan Hunter's 1954 novel, *The Blackboard Jungle*, was a year later released as a movie. Its soundtrack song, "Rock Around the Clock," seemed to many conservative North Americans to be a confirmation of the equation, rock'n'roll = delinquent teenagers. The step from *The Blackboard Jungle* to the "jukebox jungle" was a short one, and from the second half of the 1950s jukeboxes became an integral part of rock'n'roll imagery.

The manufacturers were far from comfortable with the association, and the styling change that swept through the industry with the 1955 models owed more to the hope of drawing back patrons through making jukeboxes visually exciting than to any awareness of pop-art imagery. It was in 1955 that the guru of US industrial design, Raymond Loewy, made a causative link between the two great symbols of the "flash 'fifties." However, when he posed the question, "Is it responsible to camouflage one of America's most remarkable machines as a piece of gaudy merchandise?", he was referring to the automobile, which he then went on to describe as a "jukebox on wheels."

At the time he could hardly have known that the great era during which cars and jukeboxes would meet on a plane of shared aesthetics and achieve heights (or depths) as "gaudy merchandise" was yet to come. Loewy was essentially a purist, and did not appreciate that popular design consciousness of the 1950s demanded a high entertainment value. Automobiles, in an affluent age, were a form of entertainment, and jukeboxes, by their nature, had to be obviously so – when Loewy himself eventually designed one (the 1957 United), he still had not learned that "good design" is not enough for a jukebox. The proof that something more is required had been given in 1955, when the innovators of "design" jukeboxes, Seeburg, brought out the V200, one of the flashiest jukeboxes of all time.

7 SEEBURG MEETS CADILLAC

The 1955 Seeburg V200 is a landmark in jukebox history. In terms of style, it was the flashiest of the 1950s Seeburgs. In terms of size, it was a massive machine, second only to the Wurlitzer Model 1500 for sheer bulk. In terms of technology, it was the first 200-selection jukebox, the first to feature electronic memory, and the first to incorporate dual pricing. It could also be called the last "real" Seeburg, for this was the final model brought out under the auspices of the Seeburg family, who a year later sold their interests in the company.

Records of all sorts were by now being issued in such numbers as to warrant doubling the jukebox capacity to 200 selections, particularly as AMI, Rock-Ola and Wurlitzer had started to produce machines topping the magic 100, which for so long had

given Seeburg supremacy. To increase the capacity of the changer was no problem. The Selectomatic could, in theory, be extended indefinitely, as had been proven when the mechanism first came out: a 500-selection Selectomatic had been mocked-up to show the potential of the system. The main problem was the presentation of all those extra titles. Wurlitzer had demonstrated the deadening effect of masses of title strips, yet with the Model 1100 it had produced a solution which had been adopted by Rock-Ola and which Seeburg now also picked up: the revolving title drum. Instead of the faceted drum used by Rock-Ola, where each section of titles was in a flat frame, Seeburg used a cylinder, so that the titles curved round. It was intended that the records should be divided into five categories, each having its own section of the drum: "popular hits," "old favorites," "jazz," "country and western," "polkas" and "religious music" were typical category descriptions. Extending to either side with ribbed "gold" covers, the drum took up the entire width of the machine, a dominating feature emphasized by the roundels mounted on the cabinet sides in line with it. Each roundel had a wide gold-colored band framing the center disc, which bore the name "Seeburg" on white script against a rich emerald-green background. To avoid detracting from this, the side speakers, which had a prominent porthole effect on the "R", were replaced by cooling vents behind the perforated metal that covered the entire top half of the sides. This innovative "hi-tech" look was offset by the bottom half, which was enlivened by marble-style patterns of rich green. The button bank, sloping down at the top and curving underneath toward the grille, projected out from the front to give greater emphasis to the illuminated buttons, instruction panels, and buttons. When any of these five latter buttons was pressed, the drum would revolve, stopping when the titles of

---

BELOW *The first 200-selection jukebox, Seeburg's V200 (1955).*

RIGHT *Rock-Ola's version of the "Bandshell" style was a petite, colorful and successful jukebox, the Model 1454.*

Model 1454

all the records in that category were displayed. Shining out from under the overhanging button bank was the plain mesh speaker screen, illuminated by fluorescent light beaming down through multicolored panels, the light bouncing back off four massive horizontal chrome bars.

The V200 saw the introduction of the Tormat memory unit — an electronic device that registered selections magnetically — in place of the existing electro-mechanical method. Of more impact to the patron, however, was the innovation of dual pricing. Ever vigilant to spot new directions, Seeburg had seen the trend toward EP records develop in the middle market — "all-time favorites, show tunes, classics and varieties — are principally available on EP records," as the promotional material pointed out. The problem was that the EP played for twice as long as a single. The dual-pricing system "compensated" the operator by having one price structure for the section containing EPs and another for those containing standard singles. The prices in those days were 10 cents for a single and 15 cents for an EP.

Seeburg was now deriving the benefits of having established a technological lead at the beginning of the decade. Those extra years' start meant that, while the other companies were working on their new 45rpm mechanisms (and AMI's was still a year away!), Seeburg could develop the technology of the Tormat and the dual pricing featured in the V200, as well as have the opportunity to expand its styling.

Rock-Ola and Wurlitzer were racing to catch up. Rock-Ola, having continued the 1953 "Comet Fireball" into 1954 as a "hi-fi" version (Model 1446) as well as a utility 50-selection machine (Model 1442), came up with a cabinet style which was to last it until 1959. Once again, Seeburg provided the inspiration. The Rock-Ola Model 1448 derived its large, sloping front glass, its boomerang sides (though squarer), its

ABOVE *The cabinet of the Wurlitzer Model 1800 was a radical departure from those of the 1600 and 1700 ranges.*

ribbed gold curving interior, and even its glass grille dividers and stepped chrome embellishments from Seeburg's 1954 HF100R "Bandshell." With 120 selections now standard for Rock-Ola, the 1448 was available also as a 50-play machine (Model 1452). With only minor changes, Model 1448 was carried over into 1956 as the Model 1454.

Meanwhile Wurlitzer, for whom the Model 1700 cabinet was merely on-hand housing for its new mechanism, had updated it for its 1955 Model 1800. The side profile was the same as that of the 1700 but cut off just above the carousel surround. From here glass windows curved over to meet a large chrome casting in the middle of the top. A flat front window sloped down to the point where the side glasses met the cabinet, and the line of the window continued

LEFT *An original advertisement for Rock-Ola's Model 1454.*

ABOVE *Wurlitzer's Model 1800 in production.*

sence. As a further styling feature, there was a choice of four cabinet colors.

Surprisingly, at a time when even domestic refrigerators were available in a choice of colors (including two tones), until now Wurlitzer had been the only jukebox manufacturer to make much use of color in its cabinets, and even then the Texileather options for the 1400 and 1500 series were rather drab. The biggest exponent of colored cabinets became, surprisingly, AMI. When it launched its 1955 Model F, even its hi-fi sound system took second place in the publicists' hype to the range of "spectacular" colors in which it was available:

BELOW *The X-200 record changer finally usurped the mechanism that had served AMI ever since the early days.*

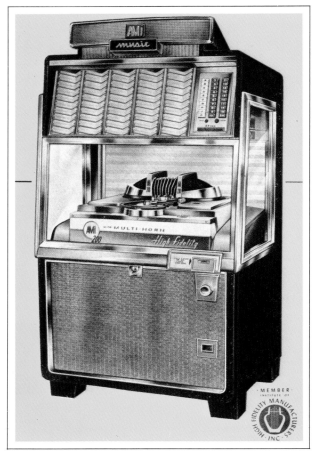

with the title-strip area and down to the button bank, which overhung the grille. The grille itself was "supported" by a pair of plastic pilasters which, instead of being in their normal position at the "edges" of the jukebox, were moved in nearly halfway toward the center. The pilasters were lined with a silver-colored sleeve featuring "cut-outs" of a rocket starburst in blues and reds. Blue light from the pilasters splashed across the speaker screen, so that the frontal effect was of rockets bursting against a metallic electric-blue sky. Set back from the front of the machine, so that the pilasters had real depth, was the speaker screen; made of textured, finely perforated ridged silver-aluminum, this was formed from two concave curves which swept in from the sides to their deepest point behind the pilasters, and then curved toward the front, where they met to form a V-shape. Although compactly styled, the Model 1800 fulfilled one of the basic requirements of a jukebox: it radiated a pre-

ABOVE *AMI's G reverted to an earlier idea, featuring an additional top-mounted speaker.*

"Color is as important to business as to life itself!" says a famous scientist. And AMI says "agreed!" Our first aim in bringing out the model "F" was to improve the automatic music business. The "F" not only delivers a new kind of automatic music – Multi-Horn High Fidelity and Sonoramic sound – but also presents this new music in a startling potent fashion – with color. "Color increases the pulse rate!" says another color authority, and what else should a new jukebox do but announce its presence with a gorgeous, streamlined cabinet rich in the newest, most dramatic colors? The "F" brings color showmanship to its theatrical peak, with a choice of eight spectacular new colors to suit every location and stimulate the public into increased music purchases. Color does the selling job, the music satisfies the customer.

AMI had judged the mood of the times correctly. Although the F cabinet showed some styling changes from that of the E – the machine was raised up on short chunky legs, the illuminated plastic had gone, and the mechanism was given greater prominence with a metal "skirt" surround – it was the innovative introduction of color that made the F the success it was: proof of the old saying that "it's amazing what a little paint will do!"

AMI's dynamism was more than just a flash in the pan. Its next series, the Gs of 1956, although basically the same in the 40-, 80- and 120-selection models, came also as a unique new machine, the G-200. AMI introduced the X-200 record changer as its first new mechanism since the A, but the A had itself been a modification rather than an innovation, and the basic changer really dated back to the 1920s! The new system was a carousel/gripper-arm combination which worked on exactly the same principle as the Rock-Ola system. As with Rock-Ola and Wurlitzer before it, getting AMI's new mechanism out onto the market had taken precedence over novel cabinet styling. Only one feature of the G-200 was to be carried over into 1957: putting the title strips in V-shaped holders to accommodate the selections

BELOW *AMI's Model F was unique in offering a complete range of colors for the cabinet styling.*

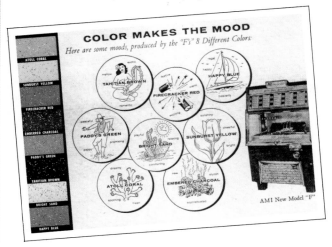

without taking up too much space. As for the rest, the 1957 models were to feature a styling quality which would put the late-1950s AMIs among the classics of the "silver age."

Nevertheless, 1956 was to be dominated by one name, and one name alone. Exactly a century had passed since Rudolph Wurlitzer had set up in business selling musical instruments in Cincinnati, and Wurlitzer was determined not to let the centenary go unnoticed. To celebrate, its two 1956 models were named the "Centennial." Taking a leaf out of the automobile industry's book, the "Centennial" was described as "custom styled":

> Styling details, high-lighted by the Centennial nameplate on the selector panel [it was actually on the frame], the colorful Wurlitzer crest on the side reproduced by skilled jewelry craftsmen, the protective metal trim around the cash box, are indicative of the custom touch that characterize this handsome instrument.

This was the beginning of an era when the jukebox appeared to be taking revenge on Loewy by drawing much of its imagery from automobiles. Wurlitzer was explicit: the cabinet was "a luxurious combination of American hardwoods and embossed metal-

ON THE **WURLITZER 2000**

TWO OR MORE PATRONS CAN SHOP THE SELECTIONS SIMULTANEOUSLY...

Tune choosing from the 200 selections on the Wurlitzer Model 2000 is fascinating fun in itself. There are 40 top tunes on the center panel – plus 20 more on each of the two roto-page "books" that flank it. A full 80 selections in sight at all times. Pages are power-turned by a finger touch on the twin illuminated bars. This novel "his" and "her" book arrangement enables two – or even more patrons to shop the program at the same time. Make-selection is an easy matter also. You press one numeral and a letter button in any sequence. All in all, this dramatic innovation has proved in itself a powerful play stimulator – one of many reasons why the Wurlitzer 2000 is boosting earning records wherever it is placed in location.

HIGHLIGHTING 100 YEARS OF MUSICAL ACHIEVEMENT

THE 200-SELECTION WURLITZER CENTENNIAL MODEL 2000

SEE IT, HEAR IT, BUY IT AT YOUR WURLITZER DISTRIBUTOR

THE RUDOLPH WURLITZER COMPANY, NORTH TONAWANDA, N.Y.

ABOVE *Wurlitzer celebrated their centennial with two "Centennial" models. Model 2000 was their first 200-selection machine.*

lized Du Pont Mylar. Highly favored today by automobile stylists for interior car trim, Mylar combines brilliant beauty with amazing wear." An even more prominent automobile influence was the wraparound mechanism window, making its first appearance on a jukebox. Wurlitzer's description of it as the "spectacular one-piece panoramic Super-Vu window" could equally well have come from a car brochure.

Stylistically, the "Centennial" models were a complete departure from the Model 1800. The back curved in, creating the Seeburg/Rock-Ola "Bandshell" effect, but the top of the canopy was dominated by a silver-and-black glass sign reading "Wurlitzer," flanked by heavy chrome castings. The "Super-Vu" window sloped down, encasing the title rack. Pilasters were returned to their rightful place at the front edges, but were now of "Swedish Modern design" glass instead of plastic. The speaker screen was in three sections, with the middle one jutting out in a V-shape. The record changer had a restyled arch,

BELOW *Two 1956 advertisements for the AMI G.*

CATCH THE **BIG** PLAY... WITH SIGHT AND SOUND

No other Juke Box is so easily serviced ...and none needs so little servicing as the new "G-200"

OVER NIAGARA FALLS

PLUS ENTERTAINMENT GALORE AT THE BIG
WURLITZER CENTENNIAL CLUB CELEBRATION
AUGUST 23-24 and 25

ALL FOR FUN
ALL FOR YOU

WURLITZER
Centennial
MODEL 1900

HIGHLIGHTING 100 YEARS OF
MUSICAL ACHIEVEMENT

SEE IT, HEAR IT, BUY IT AT
YOUR WURLITZER DISTRIBUTOR

THE RUDOLPH WURLITZER COMPANY
NORTH TONAWANDA, NEW YORK

PLUS PRIZES
BY THE HUNDREDS

ABOVE *The Wurlitzer centenary celebrations were like a return to the heady days of the 1940s. Special Wurlitzer promotions and events were run.*

which was flatter and lower, and the tone arm lost its angular functional look in favor of a graceful molded sweep.

The basic "Centennial" (Model 1900) had the standard 104 selections. The star attraction was the Model 2000, Wurlitzer's first 200-selection machine. Although the screen provided plenty of space to extend the title strips upward (a solution which Wurlitzer was later to adopt, and which was used in conversion kits for the models 2000 and 2100), this would have blocked from view part of the mechanism, and to the champions of the visible changer that would have been a design heresy. Instead, Wurlitzer staggered the title bank, with 20 double strips on static display in the center, and set back from this at the sides were a pair of "books," each with two fixed and two turning "pages" of titles. Motorized and with push-button controls, the "pages" were designed to turn, allowing access to the full array of titles. Unfortunately, this ingenious system was prone to break

down, and so conversion kits became available so that the original title area could be replaced by an entirely static display.

The centennial celebrations brought back, momentarily, the extrovert Wurlitzer image of the 1930s and 1940s. Distributors at home and overseas had "centennial parties" and participated in special promotions.

BELOW *Wurlitzer distributors all over the world held Wurlitzer birthday parties. In this illustration the Model 1900, with static title display, is featured.*

While Wurlitzer and AMI could both claim 1956 as "their" year, Seeburg and Rock-Ola relied merely on styling changes for their 1955 models. Seeburg, undergoing as it was a change of ownership, was content to "sit this one out"; the company recolored the V200's cabinet and mechanism and brought it out as the VL200. Rock-Ola restyled the front screen of the Model 1448, gave it two-toned sides, and called it the Model 1454. Although the same cabinet form was to serve them for another two years, the 1454

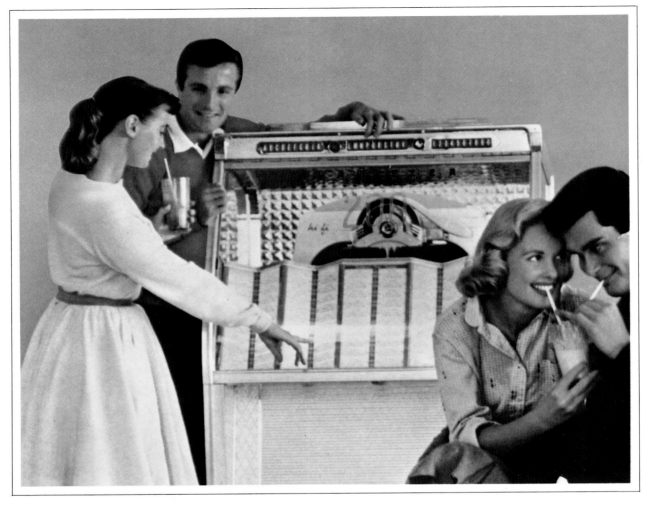

was to be their last model with an exposed record drum, glass-screened speaker front and "Bandshell" interior.

For 1957's Model 1455 Rock-Ola covered the record drum with plastic molded caps, leaving only a small gap for the gripper bow. The front was squared off and moved forward, and the grille was reduced to a simple wire mesh embellished with "gold" plastic circles, backed by a fabric speaker screen. Now with a less prominent overhang, the selector shelf lost its chrome and became wood-grained sheet metal with an illuminated window reading "Rock-Ola." Carrying 200 selections, the 1455 featured back-illuminated colored panels above the title drum, each naming the music category and embellished with an appropriate picture. The basic 1455 was designed for playing singles, but there was also a deluxe model with a dual-pricing system, allowing EPs to be played at a higher cost.

In 1957 Wurlitzer followed through its 2000 with a restyled cabinet. The Model 2100 lost the top "Wurlitzer" glass in favor of a sharper-looking valance; also, the contoured speaker screen was simplified into a greater concave of four sections. The 2100 was available with either 104 selections (Model 2104) or 200. It used title "books" in the same way as the 2000, although for Wurlitzer's other 1957 model, the 2150, these were dropped in favor of a static display. Here the obscurement of the mechanism was minimized by setting the titles lower down on the cabinet, in the area where the button bank would normally have been, the buttons being moved up to

Both the 2150 and 2250 were marketed as economy machines. The luxury models for 1958 were the 2200 (200 selections) and the 2204 (104 selections). Described by Wurlitzer as "the shape of tomorrow today," these jukeboxes have styling characteristics similar to the Wurlitzer cigarette machines of the time. Of course, the weight of a jukebox could not be supported by the tapering legs then in vogue, but, to achieve the same general effect, the cabinet was stepped in at the bottom and slightly splayed-out dummy legs were molded on. Behind these was a separate base grille. The main body of the cabinet was a squared-off U-shape in which the jukebox sat.

BELOW *With its clean lines, the AMI Model I tyified the auto-styling era of jukebox design.*

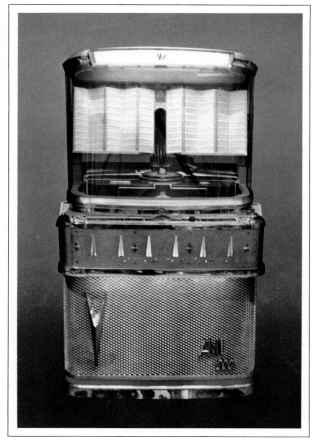

the top of the cabinet above the changer window. A further influence from AMI was the placing of the titles at angles to each other so that, except on the center column, they formed a concertina across the front of the jukebox. The cabinet was squared off and simplified, with lines on the curving front window carried through onto the side profile, so that the effect was of a continuous bow sloping back from between the sides. The speaker screen was a severely plain ribbed perforated metal.

This machine represented a radical departure from Wurlitzer's previous highly decorative models, and with slight restyling it was reissued in 1958 as the Model 2250, the main difference being the reversal of the curving changer window so that it was now concave.

ABOVE *With its flashy styling, including automobile-like fins (detail right), the Seeburg KD's youth image was affirmed in this original promotional picture.*

The buttons occupied their conventional place beneath the mechanism window, a deeply convex glass screen covering the titles, which were displayed flat for the 104-selection model, concertinaed for the 200-selection version. The interior arch was now almost completely squared off, and the carousel surround was of translucent plastic lit from beneath to bathe the changer in a soft glow. Wurlitzer claimed

that this model broke "the design barrier that has long fostered the monotony of similarity in the phonograph business," a rather overinflated idea of what was no more than a styling exercise, particularly when compared with the jukeboxes produced by AMI and Seeburg in the previous year.

Having been the "late developers" of the decade, AMI started presenting its new X mechanism in a succession of cabinets which epitomized the late-1950s look. Available with 100, 120 or 200 selections, 1957's H-series models demonstrate clear

LEFT *The AMI Model I (1958).*

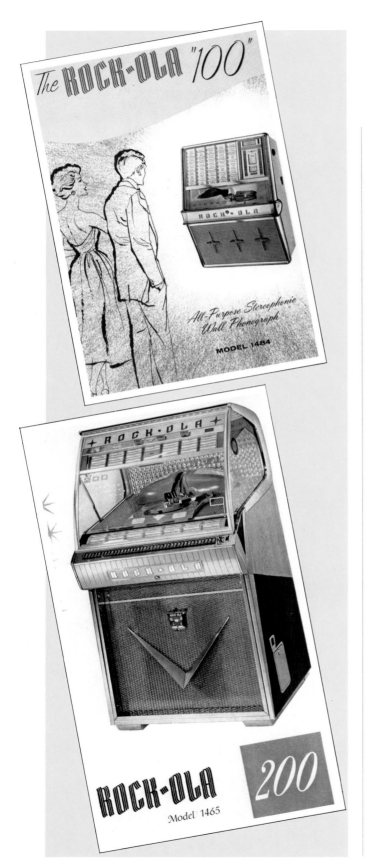

ABOVE LEFT *In 1960, Rock-Ola's Model 1484 was the successor to the original "Music Vendor."*

BELOW LEFT *The front-grille badges of the Model 1465 hinted at Rock-Ola's move toward auto-styling.*

ABOVE *The Rock-Ola "Music Vendor," Model 1464, could be mounted either on a stand or on the wall – assuming you had strong walls!*

indications of auto-styling influences. The design emphasizes height rather than width. A massive, sloping wraparound screen showed the record player and part of the carousel, surrounded by a molded dress cap, and the titles ranged across the back. (For the 100- and 120-selection versions the titles were in line; for the 200-selection version they were concertinaed.) Down-lit from a diffused fluorescent which illuminated also the glass-top valance, a narrow aperture in the titles permitted the movement of the gripper bow, so that the record came out through the titles beneath the window. The button bank jutted out and was rounded off to echo the wrap-around effect of the glass. Below, following the same lines,

RIGHT *The Seeburg Model 161 retained the fins of the KD, but dropped the revolving title drum in favor of a static display.*

was the speaker screen. A characteristic of 1950s style commonly found in automobiles and surprisingly rare in jukeboxes was the application of extraneous "bits" that detract from rather than enhance otherwise good designs, and with the Model H AMI did just that. Long arms of chrome run down the sides of the cabinet, coming forward in an L-shape to the front above the speaker screen, where they "hold" a perforated chrome light-shield. This "bumper" was removed from the following year's model, the 1958 Model I, revealing the cabinet as the perfect shape it is.

If AMI were showing the influence of the automobile, itself the most dominant styling product of its age, Seeburg had taken it one stage further in its Model K (1957), by creating a jukebox with tail lights! Three enormous vertical chrome fins spanned the plain mesh speaker screen. The fins incorporated chrome bullets, each housing a small red light. Seeburg described these bizarre designs as "jets . . . that spell beauty in motion." Quite where the jukebox was going is not clear, but probably the direction is indicated by the brochure showing a couple of teenagers playing it.

As far as automobile design went, a Ford designer has been quoted as saying "Take all the fins off and you have a piece of soap with wheels on it." Take the fins off the 1957 Seeburg K and you have an L, the economy model. It looks very empty. The Ks (single pricing) and KDs (dual pricing) were basically the same as the V series of 1955–6 but with a restyled cabinet. As in the V, the K's titles were on a revolving drum, but whereas the V had been all about flowing lines, the K reverted to the hard-edged look that had seen Seeburg into the 1950s. Not only were the front and side glasses flat, but the cabinet sides were sharply cut away. To conceal the parts of the mechanism that would normally have been shielded by the cabinet, the side glasses were screened, a feature which was to be extended throughout the rest of the 1950s Seeburgs.

By coincidence, in the same year that Seeburg and AMI incorporated automobile styling there appeared a jukebox designed by Raymond Loewy (of the famous "jukeboxes on wheels" comment). The 1957 United UPA-100 was devoid of automobile influence, but then one could hardly describe it as an interesting-looking jukebox. It nevertheless survived through the 1960s, when United was taken over by Seeburg.

The longest-serving cabinet style was that of Rock-Ola, which ended the series with two 1958 models. Both the 1458 (120 selections) and the 1465 (200 selections) were smaller than the earlier 1455. The large category panels no longer featured; instead, colored buttons in a metal frame incorporated into the lid frame were used. On the 1465 this area was extended down to include a title rack for the extra titles that could not be fitted onto the drum. The otherwise plain mesh grille of the 1458 was embellished with a mock-heraldic shield badge and four gold stars. The 1465 likewise had this, but had also a large gold "V" embellishment; this gave a hint of the auto-styling which would be a part of the next year's model.

Meanwhile, Rock-Ola also brought out a surprising specter from the 1940s, a countertop model. The 1464 120-selection "Music Vendor" was designed for smaller sites, where a full-size jukebox would be inappropriate; unlike its predecessors, however, it was not designed to sit on a counter but instead either to be mounted on a spindly-legged stand or to be fixed to the wall. The wall would have to have been a pretty substantial one, since the machine weighed in at 211 pounds (95kg), only 100 pounds (46kg) less than a full-size 1458. Styled, as the name implies, like a small vending machine, the 1464 was a complete jukebox, including speakers. The front was of wood-grained metal. Above the plain mesh speaker

RIGHT *The Wurlitzer 2300 models were among the most successful of the machines produced in the 1950s.*

THE NEW WURLITZER

MODEL 2300 200-SELECTION PHONOGRAPH

screen were the selector and category buttons, set in a plain chrome surround. A small curved window showed the mechanism and titles. Under each column of titles was a small round window with an arrow on it. When a category button was pushed, the appropriate arrow would light up, pointing to the titles in that section. Although the "Music Vendor" was not continued, the idea was resurrected in the 1960s with Rock-Ola's 1484, 403 and 430 models.

Seeburg likewise used 1958 to round off a theme. The economy model L100 was carried over as the L101, and the K200 was restyled as the Model 201 (200 selections) and the 101 (160 selections). These models retained the basic characteristics of the K, including the fins, but the glass side panels were lengthened and the revolving title drum was replaced by two static displays, one above and one below the

mechanism. The titles were now beginning to impinge on the mechanism, and the Selectomatic, which had been Seeburg's glory all through the 1950s, was barely to be seen. By mid-1958 these machines were already outdated by the new stereo 220 and 222 models.

Wurlitzer, too, was by now finding the visible changer an obstacle to styling progress. Abandoning the cigarette-machine look of the Models 2200 and 2204 consoles, for the 2300 series Wurlitzer completely reversed the features of the earlier range. Instead of being deeply curved, the window was shallow. Beneath it, on the 200-selection models, the title rack sloped backward to a metallic-blue screen that blanked off the arch. Only the top section of the changer, the record in play and the tone arm could now be seen in action. On the 104-selectors

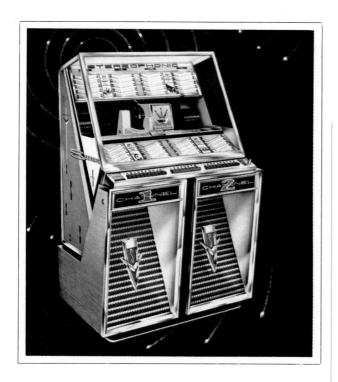

ABOVE *Seeburg's Model 220.*

the shorter title rack was blanked off. In both models the effect was the same. The window's prime function was to display the titles, with the mechanism taking a secondary role. Beneath the window frame, the button bank jutted out, the chrome extending around the sides of the cabinet in thin wedges in such a way as to exaggerate the amount by which the top half of the machine appeared to overhang the speaker screen. The screen itself, a simple wraparound of ribbed expanded mesh, was plain except for a large "gold-plated" "W" badge.

It is surely ironic that Wurlitzer, which began the 1950s with such a confused identity, should end the decade with the cleanest and yet most dynamic jukebox. Although remaining in production only for 1959, six models of the 2300 series came out: the 2300 (200 selections), the 2310 (100 selections) and 2104 (104 selections) were all mono; if the number was followed by the letter "S" the machine played in stereo.

Stereo had in fact been available since 1956. Like all the new things of the 1950s that symbolized progress toward a better and brighter future, it became immediately popular, the majority of stereo records initially being of the novelty sort specifically de-

signed to demonstrate the stereo experience to maximum effect. There were two basic reasons why it had not been used in jukeboxes before 1959. One was that, without the correct placing of the machine and the use of correct extension speakers, the effect would be lost. The other was that the majority of records now being produced were LPs, despite the fact that by 1958 teenagers, who mainly bought pop singles, accounted for 70 per cent of all record sales. The trade press of the time felt that the record industry was missing out on the "promotional" aspect of the jukebox. An article from July 1959 reads:

> With an estimated 15,000 to 20,000 stereo boxes on location throughout the US, manufacturers are losing considerable plus business. Since only 28 of the Top 100 records are available in stereo, any new stereo hit placed in the hands of distributors and one-stops where operators can get at them will be gobbled up. At the same time, record manufacturers seem to be losing sight of the tremendous promotional effect stereo singles can have on the public . . . every teenager is a stone's throw away from becoming a young adult who will want a phonograph (probably stereo) for his own home or apartment. [*The Cash Box*, July 1959.]

Undoubtedly the leader in stereo jukeboxes was Seeburg. Not only had its jukebox been the first on the market, but it had been designed around the stereo concept rather than simply adapting a conventional cabinet. As Seeburg explained,

> . . . stereo — or stereophonic — refers to the reproduction of music. But a single glance will tell you all that's necessary to know that the "222" has been designed to create an impression on the eyes as well as the ears. That's because Channel 1 and Channel 2 have been separated visually as well as functionally.

The 222 (160 selections) and 220 (100 selections) were identically styled except that on the 222 the extra titles were displayed above the changer. The twin speakers were each housed in an independent chamber, separated by a baffle. This situation was given visual impact through the use of speaker grilles. The left one, boldly marked "Channel 1" in red with a red badge on the speaker mesh, was illuminated in blue light, contrasting with Channel 2 (blue numeral and badge), which was illuminated in red light. The futuristic look was further emphasized by the cabinet sides being again lowered and the glass sides being extended downward. The general impression was that everything else was secondary to the two "channel speakers." At the same time, Seeburg also brought out a pair of extension speakers, similarly identified as "Channel 1" and "Channel 2," and furnished detailed instructions as to how the equipment should be placed for optimum effect – although it is unlikely that more than a handful of sites were ever set up "by the book," and there were hardly enough stereo singles available to warrant all the palaver.

Despite this lack of suitable discs, all the major manufacturers (and even United) were producing stereo jukeboxes by 1959. Rock-Ola introduced its new cabinet design, the "Tempo" Models 1475 (200 selections) and 1468 (120 selections), as either stereo or mono. Auto-styled much like the AMI H and I series, these featured not only the wraparound window (and auto-type badges as on the 1465) but also a button bank which had sprouted winged "fins" identical to those on the rear of the 1958 Chevrolet Impala! Pale-blue ribbed and anodized panels flanked the speaker screen and fenced off the back of the mechanism, so that as in the AMI the gripper bow plucked a record from an almost hidden carousel.

At the same time, AMI was moving away from the H and I "look." The 1959 Model J, available in

ABOVE *The electric-selection stereo version of AMI's J200.*

either mono or stereo (as well as having a choice of 200 selections in manual or electric, and 100 or 120 selections in manual), was now much squarer, with a shorter window tapering out to a massive raked-back button bank, the housing of which was carried through to the sides. To enable the window to be shortened, some of the titles now lay flat on either side of the turntable. Immediately beneath the button bank the cabinet was waisted in, before it bellied out again to accommodate a massive speaker grille. The effect of this "divided" jukebox was that the changer system seemed to sit on the speaker.

Just as the story of the 1950s really began with Seeburg's "Library System" of 1948, it ends, neatly, in 1959 with the 1,000-system Seeburg, designed to play 1,000 individual selections. The whole thing weighed little more than the 100 78rpm records used in the old 1948 system.

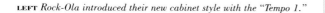

LEFT *Rock-Ola introduced their new cabinet style with the "Tempo 1."*

8 EPILOGUE

Unlike the 1940s jukebox, born from the light-up machines of the 1930s, or the boxes of the 1950s, inspired by the Selectomatic, there were no technical reasons why 1960 should bring any change to the jukebox. Apart from the emotions of entering a new decade, for the manufacturers there was no real reason why "new for 1960" should be any different from "new for 1959," and many of the images of the late 1950s were carried over into the early 1960s.

As far as Rock-Ola was concerned, the "silver age" styling of the "Tempo 1" carried it through until 1963. Its "Tempo 2" models 1485 (200 selections) and 1478 (120 selections) were distinguished by their stylized "boomerang" grille badge and by the fact that the title drum was done away with in favor of a static display.

The 1961 "Regis" – models 1495 (200 selections) and 1488 (120 selections) – incorporated some further styling changes: the button bank lost its fins and was rounded off, and the top valance was reduced in width and rounded. Nevertheless, the cabinet lines remained much the same. The "Regis" is mainly re-membered for the (mercifully brief) experiment of "Reverba-sound," a system which incorporated a re-verb unit to produce an imperceptible echo to bolster the sound. As Rock-Ola put it: "Now every location can have Concert Hall Realism. New Sound Rever-beration Technique gives vibrant living realism never before heard in recorded music for greater listening pleasure." If this "vibrant living realism" proved too much, the unit could be switched off, and there was the further facility of being able to switch from stereo to mono.

Unfortunately for Rock-Ola, recording engineers too were by now adding reverb, and the experience of a reverbed disc being re-reverbed by the jukebox was enough to convince anyone that this attempt to en-hance the jukebox sound was doomed – as indeed it was.

Last of the line was the 1962 "Empress" – models

1497 (200 selections) and 1496 (120 selections). In these the top valance was reduced to a small coin entry. By now, the design had lost all the sharpness and auto-styling relevance of the original "Tempo." It was not just the style but also the concept – the tall, dominating jukebox – which was now dated.

However, the basis of the new Rock-Ola "look" was already in existence in the form of the second-generation "Music Vendor," the 1960 Model 1484. Like the original, the 1484 was intended for floor or wall mounting, but within its compact form were all the elements which were to appear in the 1962 Model

RIGHT *The Rock-Ola "Regis," Model 1495.*

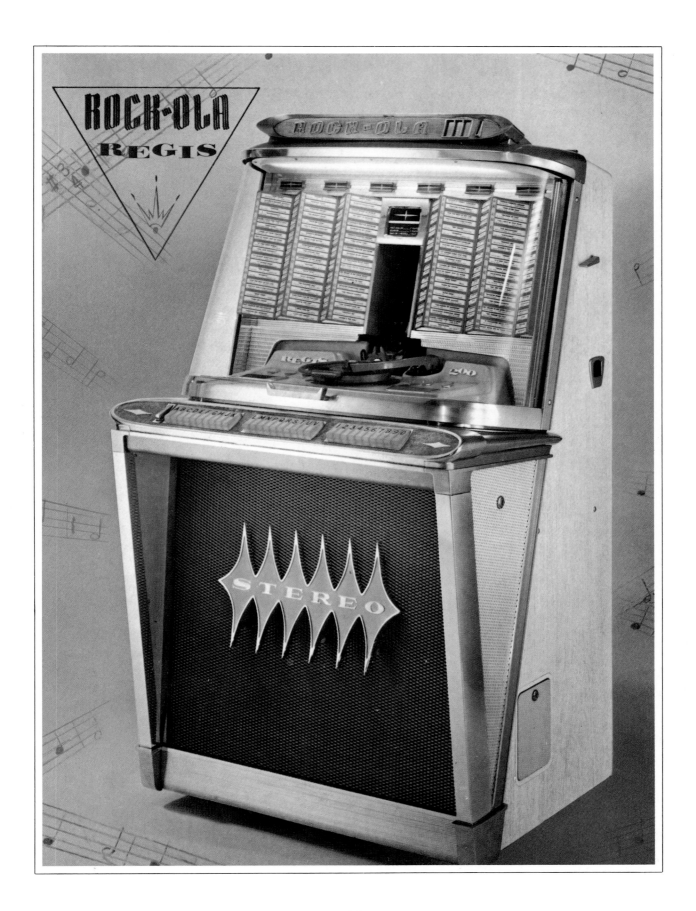

ABOVE *The "Regis" featured the short-lived experiment of "Reverba-sound."*

V-shape of another texture, framed in a chrome strip; an auto-style badge appears in the middle of the V. Further badges appear on the sides, which are finished in two-tone. The mechanism is set against a metallic backdrop with semi-relief rays of gold. The total effect is very flash, very "jukeboxy." The Model 2500 had a new dynamic, angular style and, using an extreme version of AMI's "waisted" look, separated the glassed-in top from the main body of the cabinet. This was modified into 1962's models 2600 and 2610 (200 and 100 selections respectively), to achieve a characteristic 1960s "square" look. Sticking up from the back of the box was a display panel which could show the lead titles of that site or the current Top Ten. This was used in conjunction with the machine's

BELOW *The wall-mounted Rock-Ola was to inspire the 1960s-look "Princess."*

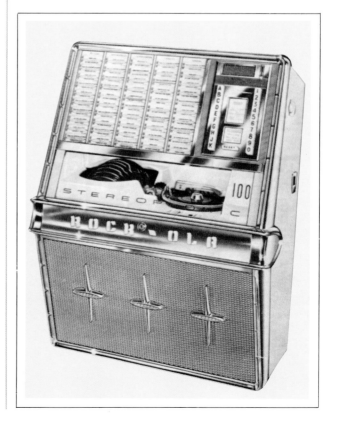

1493 "Princess." The mechanism was turned through 90 degrees, so that the carousel, instead of occupying the back of the machine, was now parallel to the sides. The changer was still on view, but now only through a narrow window. Above it, the titles and selector buttons occupied the top half of the machine. This was the foundation for a line of Rock-Olas which came to represent the basic 1960s jukebox.

As with Rock-Ola, Wurlitzer's "silver age" carried over into the 1960s, for in many ways the Model 2300 seems less 1950s than its successor, the Model 2400 (the basic 2400 had 200 selections, the 2410 had 100 selections, and the 2404 had 104 selections and was available in either mono or stereo). Whereas the lines of the 2300 are simple, those of the 2400 are complex and contradictory. The lid glass is essentially flat, but at the top incorporates a concave curve. The front grille screen is a simple wrap-around, as on the 2300, but is broken by a prominent

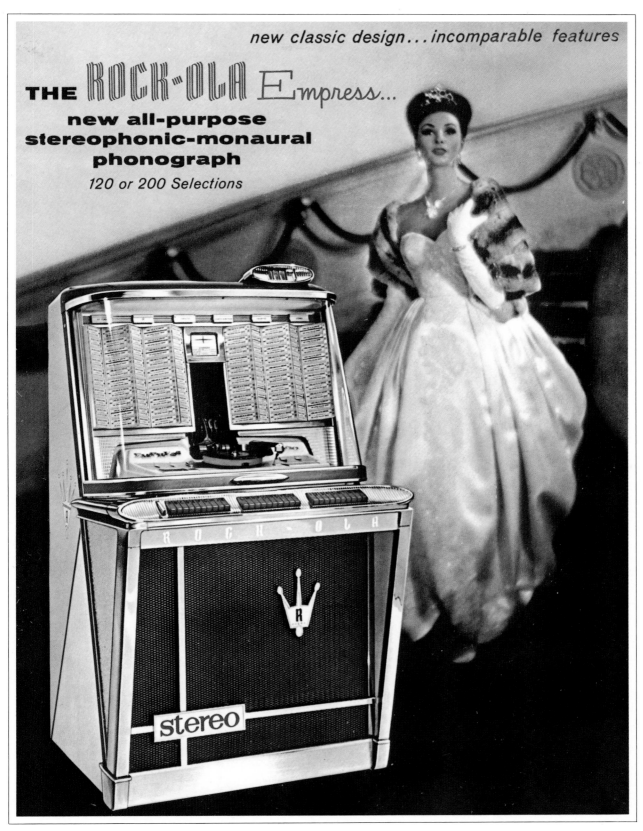

ABOVE *The Rock-Ola "Empress" was the last of the "Tempo"-shaped cabinets.*

ABOVE Rock-Ola's "Rhapsody," produced in 1964.

"Continental" was presented initially as a compact machine, and from that concept derives its unique styling. Its basic shape was of a box with a rounded back and a sloping top. To enable the record changer to be seen, a domed glass porthole rose from the top, and behind this a concave metal bracket supported the curved bank of titles.

AMI claimed that "the silhouette is unmistakably distinctive . . . truly the style of tomorrow. . . ." Futuristic it no doubt was, but after the appearance in 1961 of the "Continental 2" (available with either 100 or 200 selections, the economy version of the "Continental 1," the 100-play "Lyric," having been discontinued), the series ended. Just as it had appeared from nowhere, based on no precursors, so its successors showed no sign that it had ever existed.

popular Top Ten feature, whereby one could deposit 50 cents, push the Top Ten button, and have all of the ten records played one after the other. In styling terms, the 2600 represents the last Wurlitzer to have any link with the 1950s, for the 1963 Model 2700 replaced the angular open-look window by a sloping flat one which showed only the titles, and the changer mechanism was now completely covered over. Times had clearly changed radically for Wurlitzer: only a few years before covering the mechanism would have been regarded as heretical.

For AMI, too, 1960 represented a turning point, in that it saw the last of the line of cabinets dating back to the H. The Model K (with 200, 120, or 100 selections) was little more than a J with a restyled front. At the same time, however, the company bridged the gap between the 1950s and the 1960s with a unique design that is somehow alien to either age. The 1960

LEFT Rock-Ola's Model 1493, the "Princess."

BELOW Wurlitzer's Model 2500.

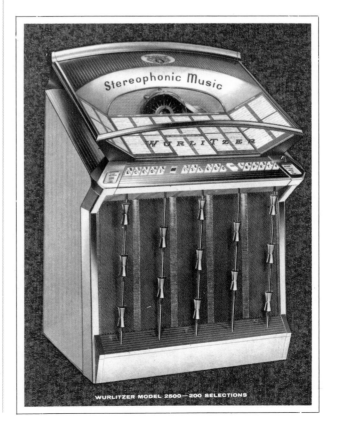

ABOVE *The Model K, produced by AMI in 1960.*

Seeburg's 1958 models 201 and 161 anticipated much of the 1960s "look." Behind the glass was a bank of titles angled almost flat across the front, with another bank across the top and the mechanism hemmed in between them. To modern eyes, the styling is definitely more 1960s than 1950s. By 1960 the Q160 and Q100 (actually brought out late in 1959) had almost lost the visible mechanism, and for the first time the Selectomatic was dropped to below the glass, so that the patron looked down at it through a narrow aperture. The rest of the glass was taken up by the titles at the top and a screened motif at the bottom; the extra titles on the 160 were shown on a vertical display at the back of the box.

For the 1960–61 AY160 and AY100 models, the flat angled glass was lowered, and the angle continued into the button bank to form a single, continuous plane. The mechanism was almost totally concealed, for the gap between the titles (now brought under the glass) was screened in a musical motif; on the AY100 model, which had only one set of titles, the screened pattern was extended. An angled illuminated speaker screen, set between the deeply concave sides of the cabinet, relieved the plainness of the overall shape.

The grille, embellished with the same profile (aside from some cosmetic changes), was carried through into 1962's DS160 and DS100 models. These, uniquely, incorporated a pair of external stereo speakers that were hinged on either side of the juke-box and were intended to produce directional sound (hence "DS").

This was the last Seeburg to have even the remotest of links with the 1950s. In August 1962 the LP (long-playing) console introduced the most radical new concept of the 1960s, having the facility to play either 33⅓rpm EPs or conventional 45rpm singles intermixed, the mechanism adjusting itself. The styling, too, was revolutionary. The cabinet was now

ABOVE AND RIGHT *The AMI "Continental" was presented initially as a compact machine. The cabinet was essentially a box with a sloping top and a rounded back, and with a domed glass porthole revealing the record changer.*

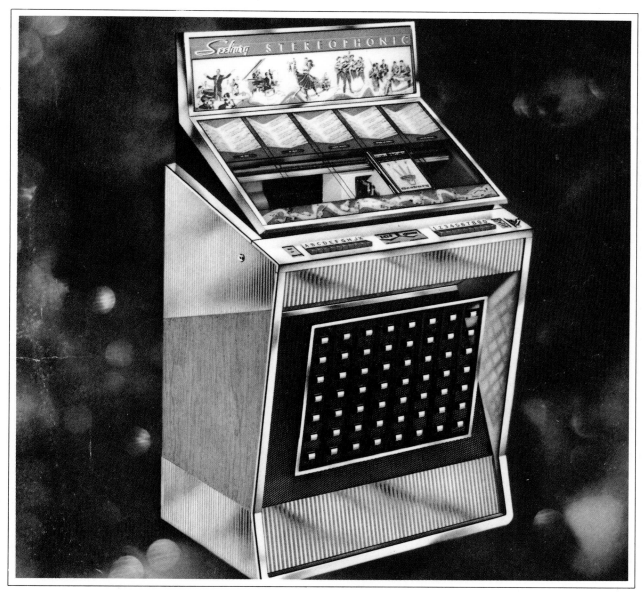

ABOVE *The Seeburg Q160 showed extra titles on a vertical display at the back of the box.*

reduced to essentials: a plain chest having the titles lying flat across the top so as totally to cover the mechanism, only the elegant upward sweep of the concave glass curving over the titles alleviating the severity. This jukebox has its own beauty, and it is important. But it belongs to a world totally alien to that of the other machines portrayed in this book.

As far as many people are concerned, the "real" jukebox died with the 1950s. Like tailfins on cars, it

embodied an age that all of a sudden seemed to be over. In a way the notion is a romantic idea — "the good die young." Publicly we mourn the tragedy, but inwardly we are gratified that these electric Dorian Grays cannot disappoint us, can never betray the promise of their youth. The 20th century needs no Grecian urn to capture time. Our images are held for us on film, on record and, by association, in the surviving products of the age. As in *Winnie the Pooh*, where somewhere a boy and his bear are forever playing, so, in some movie house somewhere, James Dean still lives; a jukebox and a little plastic disc are

LEFT *Seeburg's DS series featured hinged top speakers.*

ABOVE *Representatives of the Seeburg AY series.*

all it takes to bring Buddy Holly back to life.

These illusions falsify our history. We may get close to it, but we can never touch it. However authentic the jukebox and however mint the record, we cannot hear the music as it originally sounded, for our sensibilities have been mutated by the sounds of our own age and then further colored by the imagery and associations which we, consciously or not, bring to the experience.

Similarly, it is easy to over-romanticize jukeboxes,

to forget that whatever echoes of their era were embodied in their design – the strange beauty of the "Peacock" or the flash fins of the Seeburg – the only motivation for producing them was to create a commercially desirable piece of equipment. If we look back at the jukebox, we can see that it flourished

RIGHT *Wurlitzers are still made in Germany. The "One More Time" is a reproduction of the Model 1015, but has a modern mechanism.*

NOW—ACTUAL ALBUM MUSIC IN TRUE 33⅓ STEREO
Here is the one totally new coin phonograph that assures you the world's finest musical entertainment. New in exclusive modern styling...new in actual *album* programming. The *only* coin phonograph that plays the same 33⅓ true stereo album music your customers buy for their homes!

ABOVE *The industrial design consultants, Sundborg-Ferar Inc., of Detroit, were awarded the 1962 Industrial Arts medal by the American Institute of Architects for this cabinet, which Seeburg had commissioned. It became a modern classic.*

purely because the public wanted it. However outrageous Wurlitzer advertisements might now appear, at the time they were right. For millions, the jukebox *was* "America's favorite nickel's worth of fun."

The jukebox survived its decline in the late 1940s thanks to a life-saving injection of new technology and styling. During the 1950s, against a background of rapidly expanding consumerism and the distractions of the affluent society, the jukebox adapted itself, incorporating first 45rpm discs, then hi-fi, then the EP and, finally, stereo, constantly changing to match the moods and needs of its time.

The rate of change was incredible. From the 1946 Wurlitzer advertisements showing 1015s playing Sinatra or Guy Lombardo to those for the 1956 Seeburg K200, where teenagers are selecting Presley or

Little Richard; from the 1948 Seeburg "Industrial and Commercial Music System" providing 4–5 hours of music on 78rpm discs to 1959's 1000 system, which gave 37½ hours of listening from 25 microgroove records . . . such developments represent a rate of change that obviously could not continue.

Yet, if we accept that the "real" jukebox was born with the light-ups of 1937–8, it is now 50 years old. If we take the "silver age" to have ended in 1962–3, a full 25 years have passed since then – and still the jukebox is with us.

Or is it? Just as the pioneers in the field shunned the word "jukebox" because of its bad associations, it may be our turn retroactively to rename the "new" machines – to call them not "jukeboxes" but "coin-operated phonographs." Dr Wilheim Foelkel of Deutsche Wurlitzer wrote in 1976:

Fashion may rule angular shapes today and round shapes tomorrow and then angular again – today chromium and glass, tomorrow plain and tarnish, today baroque, tomorrow Scandinavian styling; nostalgic design today but modern lines tomorrow. Those changes will never stop neither with fashion nor with phonographs . . . even in 100 years' time people will insert coins, maybe banknotes, into a phonograph and then will select music. There will be music boxes as long as there is music . . . [*Wurlitzer News*, 1976.]

Since then, first video jukeboxes, then compact discs, have added their strata of history. Perhaps there will always be music boxes. Perhaps "music boxes" will be the name for them.

Perhaps the jukebox died the day Wurlitzer covered the mechanism over.

RIGHT *The 1973 Wurlitzer Model 1050, "Nostalgia," has since reappeared in different forms, the latest housing a Rock-Ola mechanism.*

THE WURLITZER JUKEBOX MODEL 1050

INDEX

PICTURE CREDITS

Key: *l*=left; *r*=right; *t*=top.

The majority of the pictures used in this book are from the author's collection of jukeboxes and jukebox ephemera. The author and publishers have made every effort to identify the copyright owners of the additional pictures used; they apologize for any omissions and would like to thank the following:

Page 11 *l* Sotheby's, London; page 28 *l* Ed Jones, Jukebox Junction, Des Moines, Iowa; page 27 *t* © Harold F. Tenney; page 48 *l* courtesy of Weston Gallery, San Francisco; page 48 *r* Rock and Roll Beer Company, Delmar, St Louis, Missouri; page 49 © Vintage Jukebox Company, London; page 55 *l* courtesy *Life Magazine*; page 55 *r* courtesy of *Laugh* magazine; page 59 Ed Jones, Jukebox Junction, Des Moines, Iowa; page 63 © Vintage Jukebox Company, London; page 84 courtesy of *Mad* magazine.